THE UNRESPONSIVE:

Resistant or Neglected?

THE UNRESPONSIVE:

Resistant or Neglected?

The Homogeneous Unit Principle
Illustrated by the Hakka Chinese
in Taiwan

David C.E. Liao

William Carey Library

1705 N. SIERRA BONITA AVE. • PASADENA, CALIFORNIA 91104

First published by The Moody Bible Institute, 1972
Reprinted in 1979 by the William Carey Library

Library of Congress Catalog Card Number 73-175494
International Standard Book Number 0-87808-735-4

Published by the William Carey Library
1705 N. Sierra Bonita Avenue
Pasadena, California 91104
Telephone (213) 798-0819

PRINTED IN THE UNITED STATES OF AMERICA

CONTENTS

TABLES

FIGURES

FOREWORD

As the church carries out the mandate of her Lord to disciple the nations, she continually meets unresponsive peoples. As missionaries carry the good news to the two billion who have yet to believe, they often encounter indifferent or resistant populations.

Sometimes unresponsiveness is due to hardness of heart, pride, or aloofness; but more often than we like to think, it is due to neglect. The gospel has been presented to an "unresponsive" ethnic unit in the trade language, not its mother tongue. The only church its members could join was one made up of people of a different culture. The only pastors its congregations could have were those from another ethnic unit or subculture. For example, until recently the only option open to seemingly resistant Quechua Indians in Ecuador was to hear the gospel in Spanish, join Spanish-speaking congregations of mestizos, and sit under pastors of the ruling people of Ecuador.

It is the great merit of David Liao's book, *The Unresponsive,* that it focuses attention on this church problem, commonly found in all six continents. He illustrates it by examining the Hakkas of Taiwan who number about two million, comprise the finest of the Chinese, and so far have seemed unresponsive. Mr. Liao is convinced that failure of the church to grow among the Hakkas is best explained by the facts that the Hakkas have been neglected, their language has not been learned, and they have had to join Minnan and Mandarin-speaking congregations. Consequently to them "becoming Christian" has come to mean "leaving our beloved Hakka people."

As readers from other parts of the world peruse these pages, they quickly will recognize their own neglected peoples and, I trust, will end the neglect by devising ways of communicating the gospel which channel the grace of God to those particular peoples.

Here is a book which should be read and pondered in all lands.

DONALD McGAVRAN

School of Missions
Fuller Theological Seminary

PREFACE
To the Second Edition

"WHY IS THE CHURCH among the Hakka Chinese in Taiwan so much smaller than those among the other language groups on the island?" That was my question when I first embarked upon the field research for a dissertation done under the mentorship of Dr. Donald A. McGavran at the Fuller School of World Mission, California.

As I proceeded along, however, I was more and more intrigued by the subject, and decided to comb through all available literature sources to produce a comprehensive study, including the history and the culture, of this peculiar branch of the Chinese race. The result was this book, which has become a documented illustration for the Homogeneous Unit Principle in missionary approach.

As the Homogeneous Unit Principle is now gaining increasing recognition in missions circles, there is also an increasing demand for this book, formerly published by Moody Press. I am grateful that William Carey Library has reprinted it to meet such a need.

1

RESISTANT PEOPLES—A
WORLDWIDE PHENOMENON

EVER SINCE THE APOSTLES of Jesus Christ began to
preach the gospel and plant churches, Christianity has met
with different kinds of response among different peoples.
Paul met responsive Bereans side by side with resistant
Thessalonians (Acts 17). Throughout the entire history of
Christian missions, such a situation has continued to exist.
Any student of modern Christian missions will be curious to
find out, for instance, why the evangelicals constitute 10
percent of Chile's population, while in Peru the percentage is
only 1.2. Why, again, does Burma have 3.3 percent
Christians, while Thailand has only a tiny 0.1 percent?

Those who are familiar with these countries can immediately point out that political divisions are very
inadequate units for the calculation of Christian percentages,
because the population of one nation often contains a
number of different races, tribes, castes, or linguistic groups.
It would be more accurate to talk in terms of these natural
units with regard to their responsiveness to the gospel. These
subdivisions, each with its own distinctive culture, may
respond to the gospel in vastly different ways — some very
responsive, some very resistant. Thus in Burma, instead of
seeing the entire population as simply Burmese, we can see
the highly responsive Karen tribespeople as compared to the
much less responsive lowland Burmese. Karen Christians
actually constitute a large portion of the total Christian
community in Burma. Or, in Liberia, instead of seeing a

general populace of Liberians, we can see the high Christian percentage among the minority of English-speaking Americo-Liberians, in contrast to the tiny Christian elements among the tribal Liberians who make up 90 percent of the nation's population. The fact that both groups are Negroes by no means minimizes the big cultural difference between them.

A GREAT PUZZLE IN MISSIONS

Just why some of these ethnic groups are more resistant than others is a great puzzle in missions. As the church carries out the Great Commission throughout the world, she continually runs across such resistant groups. Some peoples or sections of a people seemingly reject the gospel. The church fails to take root and multiply among them. What can we do about it? We may say these peoples are too hard-hearted, too idolatrous. Apparently God's time has not yet come for their salvation. After all, we have already given them a gospel witness; what more can we do except to leave them in God's hands?

But a conscientious servant of God cannot dismiss the problem so quickly with ready-made answers. To be sure, some peoples are truly resistant; but many are not. Resistance has a variety of possible causes. Sometimes an ethnic group is resistant in one country but responsive in another. Or, a people may be resistant with regard to certain denominations of the church but responsive with regard to other denominations. It is important, therefore, to ascertain whether the resistance shown by a particular group is due to an inborn hostility to the gospel, or to faulty procedures in evangelization and church planting. As we look at the members of a resistant group, we must first ask: Are they resistant no matter what has been done, or is their resistance merely a reaction against our inadequate attitude toward them? Have we used the very best ways to understand and win them?

Examples can be found from the worldwide mission fields to support the assumption that a difference in approaches often causes a difference in responsiveness. One cannot imagine, for example, that theology has much to do with the fact that in Jamaica during the early 1800s, plantation owners were Anglicans and Presbyterians, mulattoes were Methodists, and Negroes were Baptists. The difference was largely in the mission approaches and policies.

Another example can be found in Chile where a certain mission with some thirty missionaries has worked among a people for over forty years. They have some twenty congregations with a total of 239 members. They feel the growth of their churches — in this highly resistant land — is extremely difficult. But actually the reason for their tiny membership is that they spend a very large portion of their resources in educational work and expect individual young students to become Christians. Meanwhile, another mission using other methods among the same people is getting good growth. This shows that this particular segment of Chile's population is not resistant at all. The first mission does not have growth because its methods are inadequate. Therefore, when our own church is static in a given field while churches of other denominations are growing by leaps and bounds, it is time for us to examine ourselves to see whether we have inadvertently by erroneous approaches and policies missed the very people whom we have come to win. The awareness of God's sovereignty in calling and saving certain peoples by no means precludes our responsibility of placing our best in God's hand to reach them. To judge a people hastily as being resistant and then become satisfied with little growth, is poor stewardship on our part.

RESISTANCE AS A SYMPTOM OF NEGLECT

In many cases, resistance is no more than a symptom of neglect. We in mission circles think we have neglected no people in the world. Do we not have missions capitalizing on "new tribes" so as not to leave a single ethnic unit untouched? Do we not have translation and publishing agencies whose sole purpose is to provide a Bible in every tongue under the heavens? Do we not have some forty thousand missionaries scattered in all corners of the world to welcome every human being into the church of Jesus Christ?

Neglect can exist, however, in subtle forms. One common form, for example, is to underestimate the importance of cultural differences. This often happens in the case of bilingual minorities of a country. If the church has first been established in the majority group, then it is likely that the minority, who usually learns to speak the language of the majority group as a trade language, will be asked to become Christians within the majority culture. The new, young churches of the minority are made to struggle under rules designed for strong churches of the majority. Often the minority resents such arrangement and shows signs of resistance. They reject the Christian religion, not because they dislike it, but because they do not want to be swallowed up by another culture.

THE HAKKAS AS AN EXAMPLE

The Chinese Hakka people in Taiwan provide an interesting illustration of this point. The Hakkas in Taiwan number 1,700,000 and constitute 13 percent of Taiwan's total population. Racially and culturally, they are among the finest of pure Chinese. In fact, they have been called the cream of the Chinese people. Being descendants of northern Chinese with a long and honorable history, the Hakkas speak their own language and retain enough of their peculiar identity to form a distinctive group. The word *Hakka* means "household of sojourners", a designation of which these rugged mountaineers are proud. The main bulk of the Hakka population, estimated at 10,000,000, dwell in their old settlements in Kuangtung province of south China. It was a Hakka who led the Taiping movement a century ago and nearly overthrew the Manchu dynasty. Dr. Sun Yat-sen also, who did overthrow the Manchu dynasty and founded the Republic of China in 1912, was a Hakka descendant.

For years in Taiwan, the Hakkas have had the reputation of being resistant to the Christian gospel. The percentage of Christians among them is conspicuously lower than that of other subcultural groups. Are they truly resistant?

Burdened over the stagnant condition of the small Hakka church, the writer began to do some investigation. The result was surprising. Contrary to the common belief, the Hakkas are not resistant — but they have been neglected. This finding has prompted the writer to do more investigation and to contemplate more seriously the problem of resistant peoples elsewhere.

The thesis of this book is: Many seemingly resistant peoples in the world, like the Hakkas, are really being neglected. Throughout the book, the Hakkas in Taiwan will be used as a long, extended illustration of the thesis. As we enter into a depth study of the Hakkas, we hope a flood of light will be cast upon the propagation of the gospel all over the world among other allegedly "resistant" peoples. All are not like the Hakkas; nevertheless, as we see the Hakkas and investigate closely their condition, we shall come to understand many "resistant" peoples.

In this book, the writer is attempting to answer questions such as the following: Why are the Hakkas supposed to be resistant? Have they been resistant under every circumstance? Has the church in Taiwan neglected them? What will have to be done to win them to Christ?

Inquiries are made into the background and development of their strong sense of group identity, which seems to present the key to an accurate understanding of their problems, and to the formulation of an effective approach to this great people. One chapter is devoted to the crucial issue of ancestor worship, which is a well-known obstacle to the evangelization of the Chinese in general, and the Hakkas in particular.

The writer has served for more than fifteen years in Taiwan with Overseas Crusades, Inc., an interdenominational mission serving existing churches in the fields of evangelism and training of Christians. He therefore has wide contacts with both foreign missionaries and national churchmen. In order to obtain basic information for this book, a careful field survey was conducted in the fall of 1968. The survey consisted first of all in a questionnaire of which 239 copies were sent to all churches in predominantly Hakka areas all over Taiwan. The purpose of this questionnaire was to survey the general condition of the churches and the local population, as well as to invite opinions from ministers concerning the evangelization of the Hakkas. A total of 137 questionnaires were returned.

The writer then traveled extensively throughout Hakka

areas in Taiwan, mostly in the hilly regions, to visit the chief Hakka congregations and to interview about sixty ministers and missionaries to find out what they think about the situation and to discuss with them the problem of church growth among the Hakkas. About forty Hakka Christians were also interviewed in order to understand their conversion patterns and relationships to nonchristian family members.

This book is now sent forth with the prayer that ministers and missionaries in many lands will read it (seeing in it a description of the ethnic groups to which the Great Shepherd sends them) and ask the same question: *Resistant — or neglected?*

2

HAKKAS—THE MOST "RESISTANT" PEOPLE IN TAIWAN

The Four Ethnocultural Groups

THE THIRTEEN MILLION PEOPLE on the island of Taiwan can be divided into four ethnocultural groups as shown in figure 2.1. Besides a small minority of tribal Highlanders, the ethnic Chinese population is made up of three distinctive subcultural groups: — the Mainlanders, the Minnans, and the Hakkas. (See App. B for details.)

Fig. 2.1. Composition of Population in Taiwan

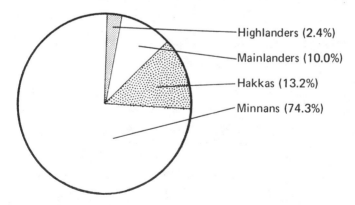

Highlanders (2.4%)
Mainlanders (10.0%)
Hakkas (13.2%)
Minnans (74.3%)

The Highlanders, in seven major tribes, are ethnically related to the Malayo-Polynesian races. They have lived on the island of Taiwan since time immemorial. Since the arrival of Chinese immigrants (ca. A.D. 1660), these Highlanders have been gradually pushed from the coastal plains to the high mountain ranges which run through the whole length of the island. They live in aboriginal villages and retain much of their own culture.

The Mainlanders, Minnans, and Hakkas are ethnic Chinese. They all came from mainland China but in different periods of history and therefore formed different subcultures. The Mainlanders, the latest newcomers, began to arrive in 1945 when Taiwan was returned to China from Japan; but the main bulk of them crossed the strait in 1949 when the Chinese Communists overran the mainland. These Mainlanders, dispersing throughout the whole island, are a conglomeration of people from all parts of mainland China. Most of them speak Mandarin, China's official language, with some regional variations.

Both the Minnans and the Hakkas are native lowland Taiwanese. The Minnan people originally came from the province of Fukien in south China. (Therefore they are also called *Hoklos* — the fellows from Hokkien, or Fukien. This term *Hoklo* was commonly employed by all earlier writers, and is still in colloquial use in Taiwan. Being the majority group on the island, they are often referred to simply as "Taiwanese." However, the exact and standard designation for them is "Minnan" — southern Fukien.) While they have been moving to Taiwan since the fifteenth century, the largest migration took place in 1661 when General Cheng Ch'eng-kung (Koxinga) brought thousands of his Minnan compatriots to recover the island from the Dutch who occupied Taiwan during 1624—1661. The Minnans, who speak the Minnan language (also known as Amoy), have since become the major stream of life in Taiwan.

The Hakka people came from the province of Kuangtung in south China and speak the Hakka language. Their migration to Taiwan was somewhat later than that of the Minnans. They inhabit largely the foothill regions of the island, and form communities of their own.

CHURCHES IN THESE FOUR GROUPS

The total Protestant community in Taiwan numbers three hundred eighty thousand and constitutes 2.9 percent of the total population. But when the Christians are divided according to the four ethnocultural groups as shown in figure 2.2, a striking fact is that the church among the Hakka people is far smaller than those among the other three groups. (See App. A for details.)

Fig. 2.2. Sizes of Protestant Communities
in Taiwan
(1967)

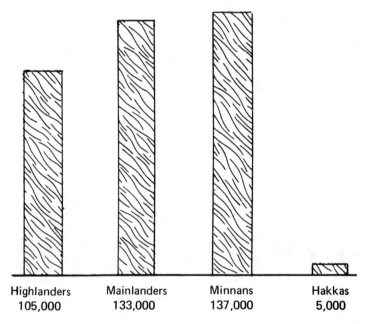

Highlanders	Mainlanders	Minnans	Hakkas
105,000	133,000	137,000	5,000

Since the four groups of population are of unequal size, the true picture can better be seen by comparing the percentage of Christians in each ethnocultural group:

Highlanders . . . . 33.3% Protestant
Mainlanders . . . . 10.1% Protestant
Minnans . . . . 1.4% Protestant
Hakkas . . . . 0.3% Protestant

Now we see that the Highlanders have very much the highest percentage of Protestant Christians, and the Hakkas very much the lowest.

TABLE 1

PERCENTAGES OF LOWLAND PRESBYTERIANS IN POPULATION (1965)

Approximate Division of Presbytery	Administrative Divisions	Population	Lowland (Minnan & Hakka) Presbyterian Community	Percentage in Population	Comparison of Percentage by Graph
Eastern	Taitung county	247,082	1,697	0.69	
	Hualien county	284,962	3,212	1.1	
Ch'i-hsin & Taipei	Yilan county	368,550	1,586	0.43	
	Keelung city	263,073	1,015	0.39	
	Taipei city	1,058,595	6,055	0.57	
	Taipei county	1,113,375	5,071	0.46	
Hsinchu	Taoyuan county*	556,662	1,195	0.22	
	Hsinchu county*	510,319	1,044	0.21	
	Miaoli county*	469,301	1,329	0.28	
Taichung	Taichung city	341,451	2,063	0.61	
	Taichung county	665,082	2,691	0.40	
	Nantou county	452,580	3,539	0.78	
	Changhua county	950,349	9,146	0.96	
Chiayi	Yunlin county	726,847	4,156	0.57	
	Chiayi county	770,451	6,266	0.81	
Tainan	Tainan city	380,707	7,108	1.9	
	Tainan county	848,369	12,026	1.4	
Kaohsiung & Pingtung	Kaohsiung city	551,213	9,746	1.8	
	Kaohsiung county	683,539	9,978	1.5	
	Pingtung county	715,157	9,983	1.4	
	Penghu county	107,427	1,641	1.5	

*Predominantly Hakka areas.

SOURCE: Data from Tze-shih Chung, *Basic Plans and Study Materials for the Second Century of the Mission*, pp. 83-103.

The Highlanders, who used to be headhunters, were miraculously Christianized during the years 1940 to 1960. Most of these Highland Christians are Presbyterians and Roman Catholics. Their story is certainly an interesting one that forever sings praise to our Saviour, but it lies beyond the scope of this book.

Being war refugees, the Mainlanders have been very open to the gospel, especially during the decade 1949—1959. A great many missionaries, when expelled from the mainland, came to Taiwan to work among them. This accounts for their higher percentage of Christians. These mainland believers form the chief part of some forty large and small denominations established during the years 1949 to 1959.

THE WEAKEST PRESBYTERY

The church among the native Lowlanders (i.e., the Minnans and the Hakkas) has a longer history. The gospel was brought to Taiwan as early as the seventeenth century by Dutch missionaries. When Dutch rule was replaced by Chinese, however, Christianity was quickly stamped out. In 1865 the gospel entered Taiwan again with the arrival of English Presbyterian missionaries. Later they were joined by colleagues from the Canadian Presbyterian mission. For sixty years the Presbyterians remained the only Protestant church on the island. It was not until the 1920s that the holiness church was introduced from Japan, and the True Jesus Church (an indigenous Pentecostal church) from mainland China.

Today, the Presbyterian church is by far the largest church among the Minnans and the Hakkas. Yet the Hakka membership is markedly smaller than the Minnan. The percentages of lowland Presbyterians in population, according to 1965 statistics, are listed in Table 1.

It is obvious that the percentages for the three predominantly Hakka counties — Taoyuan, Hsinchu, and Miaoli, each marked with an asterisk — are smaller than those for the Minnan areas. Hsinchu presbytery, consisting of churches in these three counties, is the weakest of the nine lowland presbyteries.

WHY SUCH A TINY HAKKA CHURCH?

Why in any country do some sections of the population seem so hard to Christianize? Churchmen can give a wide variety of answers. Whatever the analysis may be, one frequent tendency is to point out the hardheartedness of the people in question.

Why in Taiwan do the Hakka areas have the lowest percentages of Protestant Christians? Tabulated on table 2 are the answers given by ministers on the questionnaires sent out as a part of the field survey conducted by the writer in the fall of 1968. (See App. D for questionnaire form.) The respondents were asked to write down their own analysis and opinions as to why the growth of Hakka church is so slow and hesitant. One person could give as many reasons as he felt necessary. Out of the 137 forms returned, 105 ministers gave substantial answers classified in the table.

The answers are listed in two groups: *A*, those having to do with inadequacies of church and mission; and *B*, those having to do with the Hakkas. Certainly both groups of factors which will be dealt with in the following chapters have contributed to the retarded growth of the Hakka church. But here it is sufficient to note that the objective factors (group B) are mentioned almost three times more frequently than the subjective factors (group A). The "resistance" of the people is in the foreground of the thinking of most churchmen. Shall we agree with them? Before we give the name "resistant" to the Hakkas or to any other peoples, let us first look at some evidences to the contrary.

TABLE 2

REASONS FOR DIFFICULT CHURCH GROWTH IN HAKKA AREAS

ANSWERS	FREQUENCY			
	From 26 Ministers of Hakka Presbyterian Congregations	From 31 Ministers of Hakka Congregations of Other Denominations	From 48 Ministers of Non-Hakka Congregations	Total (105 Ministers responded)
A. Failures of the Church:				
Lack of Hakka-speaking church workers	8	5	16	29
Lack of specialized efforts for evangelizing Hakkas	9	3	4	16
Financial weakness (because Hakkas are poor and stingy)	10	4	5	19
Total				**64**
B. Characteristics of Hakka culture which obstruct church growth:				
Conservatism	16	17	15	48
Idol worship	11	5	14	30
Ancestor worship	8	11	15	34
Tight control by lineage groups	8	11	9	28
Stubbornness, self-assertion, exclusiveness	7	6	6	19
Emphasis on material gain only	2	6	6	14
Total				**173**

3

THE RESPONSIVE HAKKAS

THROUGHOUT THE WORLD, much evidence points out that some seemingly resistant peoples can be quite winnable under certain situations. The Maya Indians, for example, are generally resistant in Guatemala but responsive in Mexico. Can this same idea be true of the Hakkas? In this chapter, we will examine a few favorable evidences for them. Readers may think of other supposedly resistant populations in other countries and furnish similar evidences.

SOLID PROGRESS OF THE HAKKA CHURCH ON MAINLAND CHINA

Since the Hakkas in Taiwan are immigrants from the Hakka areas in the Kuangtung province of south China, it will aid understanding to examine how the church grew among the Hakkas there.

The Hakkas are one of the three major ethnic groups in Kuangtung province. The southeastern coastal area, including the two large cities of Ch'aochou and Swatow, is inhabited by immigrants from southern Fukien, and therefore they are called Hoklos in Kuangtung province. Toward the center, south, and west are the Cantonese, the largest ethnic group, who were the first Chinese to settle in Kuangtung. Hence they are called Puntis — the natives. The Hakkas came from Fukien and Kiangsi provinces at a much later time and settled in the mountainous northeastern corner of the province. They number several millions and constitute one sixth of the total population in Kuangtung province.

The early missionaries in south China found the Hakka people responsive. One writer said that "from a missionary point of view they are more accessible than the Cantonese."[1] Another said, "The Hakka are approachable for Christian teaching . . . . There has not been wanting a proportion of Hakka who have taken the Gospel to their hearts, and there are many instances of deep-rooted piety in those of the second and third generations."[2]

The missionary work in the Hakka areas was pioneered by German missionaries, followed by others from Britain and America. Within seventy years, these missionaries saw a Hakka church of thirty thousand souls firmly established.

BEGINNING OF CHURCH PLANTING BY GERMAN MISSIONARIES

In 1846 Charles Gutzlaff, the well-known missionary to China, made an urgent call in Europe for workers to penetrate inland Kuangtung where no missionary work was being done at that time. In response to this call, four young missionaries were sent to China. Gutzlaff divided up the province of Kuangtung among them. The two men from the Rhenish Mission took up the work among the Cantonese; and the other two, from the Basel Mission, Theodore Hamberg and Rudolf Lechler, were entrusted with the responsibilities for the Hakkas and the Hoklos respectively. After five years of difficult labor under strong opposition in Swatow among the Hoklos, Lechler finally joined Hamberg in Hakka work. Therefore these two men, the first missionaries sent out by Basel Mission, were the founders of the Hakka church. The Basel Mission was a Hakka mission from the very beginning.

Stationed in Hong Kong, Hamberg started to work among the Hakkas at Pukak village just beyond the Kowloon border. In 1852, a second station farther inland was opened at Lilong village in San-on county, when Hamberg visited there for three weeks and baptized twenty persons before he left. Prior to that, a man from that village came in contact with Hamberg in Hong Kong and believed. When he went back home, he brought a number of relatives to the Lord before Hamberg's visit.[3]

Another Hakka man, born in Ch'ang-loh county, became a

Christian in Hong Kong. After a training for preaching, he went back to his own place, and by 1860 "the number of honest seekers after truth was about 200." Thrilled by the news, another Basel missionary, Winnes by name, hurried to Ch'ang-loh — at the risk of deportation, since he carried no passport. He taught the converts, and baptized a hundred persons on two successive Sundays. When Lechler visited Ch'ang-loh again in 1863, "What a joyful event was his appearance to the poor and oppressed Christians who were living in sixteen different villages!" Lechler baptized thirty-eight persons during that trip.[4]

THE STEADY GROWTH OF BASEL MISSION

Thus the Lord led them to move farther and farther inland ("up-country"), and by 1906 the Basel Mission had fifteen stations and eighty outstations (eighteen in the low-country and *sixty-two* in the mountains) in all the important county seats and market towns of Hakkaland, including, of course, the most populous cities of Kaying and Hsing-ning. The communicant membership for 1905 in the Basel Mission was 5,691 (all Hakkas).[5]

The Basel missionaries itinerated widely in "the surrounding villages proclaiming the gospel in schools, temples, and private houses." In the towns, they had preaching halls. They "considered it their first and most

TABLE 3
GROWTH OF THE CONGREGATIONS IN BASEL MISSION
(1878–1923)

On January 1st:	Head-Stations	Out-Stations	European missionaries	Chinese missionaries	Ordained ministers	Christians	Communicants
1878	4	15	10	2	—	1,627	1,048
1885	8	22	12	4	3	2,721	1,611
1895	13	32	21	4	1	4,071	2,504
1905	15	86	32	1	4	8,530	5,914
1914	19	115	41	—	11	12,185	7,978
1924	18	135	28	—	23	15,463	8,816

important duty to preach the Gospel among the heathen." They always took Chinese preachers along when they traveled, and where a group of Christians gathered, there a catechist was stationed to pastor them. The main duty of such catechists, however, was still to preach the gospel to the non-Christians. Besides preaching and church planting, the missionaries also operated schools, hospitals, and a theological seminary. [6]

The healthy growth of the Hakka church planted by the Basel Mission can be seen from table 3, taken from one of the books written by missionary Wilhelm Oehler. [7]

In general, the German missionaries found that "in the up-country better progress is observed . . . ." [8] This meant regions in the heart of Hakkaland. In the low-country, the coastal areas near Hong Kong, church growth among the Hakkas was seriously hampered by a large amount of emigration to Southeast Asia. However, the Basel missionaries succeeded in helping some of these migrating Christians organize churches in their new homes. In Basel statistics for 1905, for example, was listed a Hakka Christian community of 399 souls (223 communicants among them) in North Borneo. [9] The writer was told by Stanley Benson, a missionary of the Lutheran Church of America, that he worked among this community in the early 1950s. He described this Hakka church in North Borneo as being active, indigenous, and self-reliant. Also, we find that the Basel Mission established a station in Singapore, probably in the first decade of this century, at the urgent request of the Hakka Christians who had migrated there. "Sixteen hundred Christians were gathered in before the War." [10]

THE ENGLISH PRESBYTERIAN MISSION AND THE
HAKKA PRESBYTERY

The work of the English Presbyterian Mission in China was begun in 1847 when William C. Burns entered the Amoy section of Fukien province. In 1856 he moved to Swatow to carry forward the churches among the Hoklos, left by Lechler in 1852. "The Hakka country to the west of the district was touched at an early stage." The first Hakka station was opened in 1870 at Wukingfu, a village sixty miles west of Swatow. The growth of the Hakka churches was so encouraging that the English Presbyterian Mission deemed it wise to start a separate Hakka division. Therefore in 1881, a center was set up at Wukingfu to take charge of all existing Hakka congregations and to develop others in Hakka areas bordering the region occupied by the Basel Mission.

Starting with 190 communicants in 1881, the English Presbyterian Hakka Mission enjoyed a steady growth, quite independent of the Hoklo Mission at Swatow. *All work was carried out in the Hakka language.* Another station was soon added at Sam-lo in north Hakkaland. By 1904 the Hakka Mission had two stations (with missionaries), thirty-nine congregations (among them thirteen were organized) with 989 communicants and a Christian community of 1,565. These Hakka congregations formed the Wukingfu Presbytery, linked with the Hoklo Christians through the synod. At Wukingfu were seminary, hospital, and boys' and girls' schools. Donald MacIver and William Riddle were among the Hakka-speaking missionaries of the English Presbyterian Mission. [11]

TESTIMONY OF AN OPIUM SMOKER

In his book *THE "STRANGER PEOPLE,"* English missionary W. Bernard Paton wrote about the Hakka people and the encouraging growth of the church among them.

> An opium smoker, a Hakka, hearing of the wonderful cures wrought in our Mission hospital at Swatow, resolved to go and put them to the test in his own person. He went, and while there not only found release from his opium habit, but heard the preaching of the Gospel. Report hath it that the words which held him were: "The blood of Jesus Christ, His Son, cleanseth from all sin." He was at the time out in the open having his head shaved, and happened to overhear some one preaching. He rushed forward, half-shaven as he was, saying: "Is that true? Is that true?" And being assured of the truth of the message, he bought two Gospels, printed in Chinese. On his return to his Hakka home, he and his wife began to pray for the coming of the missionaries to their own district.

If this be the man I believe it to be, it was his influence that led to the opening "on trial" of the station at Sa-pa-kong. His widow died at the great age of ninety-one, blind, but a bright and attractive personality of strong Christian character. His son was ordained to the ministry, and was for many years in charge of one of our Hakka congregations. Three of his grandsons passed through our Mission High School. All are members of the Church. One is now a teacher in a Government school; another training to become a Christian doctor; and a third, having won a Government scholarship, recently completed five years' training in an American university, and will doubtless, in the days to come, be a healthy and a powerful influence in the moulding of his country's future. Surely a modern illustration this of the Apostolic experience that "mightily grew the word of God and prevailed."[12]

HAKKA CHURCH REACHES OUT TO THE NEIGHBORING PROVINCE

Paton also wrote about the missionary outreach made by the Hakka church itself. The account quoted below gives one the impression of a lively, indigenous church — the result of the labor of Hakka Christians:

The Hakka Church is not content only to maintain and develop her own inner Life. She is also looking out upon regions still uncared for, and, with the Swatow brethren through the native Synod, organising and supporting a mission of her own. The field specially assigned to the Hakka Church is in the neighbouring province of Kiang-si, where five stations have now been established, being manned and financed by the native Church. There is large opportunity for a forward move in this field. The Rev. R. W. R. Rentoul, after visiting in this region in 1922, gives the following account of his reception:

"I have been in every one of the stations in Kiang-si, including Fui-chhong, where no European has been for twelve or more years. My reception there was truly impressive. We did thirty miles that day, arriving near the city at 8:30 p.m. About six stalwart Chinese, young and middle-aged, met us with picturesque Chinese lanterns, hanging from the ends of short sticks. From there on, for about one and a half miles, we gradually met and added to our numbers groups of two or four, who were waiting, some with road lamps, some with Chinese lanterns. The people with good road lamps were told to fall in, some in front and some behind me, so that the procession became a long line of dim Chinese lanterns, waving to and fro, whose centre was a 'Pastor,' vividly thrown up in the full glare of all the road lamps. When we got to the city they made me get into the sedan chair, and from that gate for about a mile to the church the din of crackers was incessant, the smoke became thick and the glare of lanterns lurid. The yells of children, the talk and gabble of the crowd (nearly the whole city turned out and hundreds lined the road on either side; while at cross roads there were great masses of people), the smoke, the dimly lit streets, the fierce fizzing and banging of crackers, all combined to make the scene weird in the extreme. At the church the crowd was dense. Fortunately they did not take long to clear away. They proved to be very nice people on the whole, and contributed quite a creditable sum to the British & Foreign Bible Society."[13]

BERLIN MISSIONARY SOCIETY

Berlin Missionary Society also began its work among the Hakkas. Its missionaries A. Hanspach and F. Hubrig arrived in 1856 and 1866. They started in the Hong Kong area and gradually developed toward inland Kuangtung and even over into Kiangsi province. In 1905 this mission had twenty-one stations and 5,442 communicant members. Evangelism through missionary itinerating was considered most important. In order to remove suspicion on the part of the local people, Hanspach established 150 village schools in just a few years.[14] By 1922 this mission had expanded into twenty-eight stations and 230 outstations forming a network of churches reaching its entire field in the northern part of Kuangtung.[15]

OTHER MISSIONS

The American Baptist Mission had a Hakka department with a station in Kaying established in 1907.

The Church Missionary Society had work among the Hakkas in the vicinity of Hong Kong and Canton for many years.

The Wesleyan Methodist Mission had one station at Ying-tak.[16]

The London Missionary Society had one station at Pok-lo established in 1861 as a result of a native Christian suffering martyrdom for his faith.[17]

The Southern Baptist Convention had one station at Ying-tak and fourteen outstations.[18]

TOTAL COUNT OF HAKKA CHRISTIANS

Oehler considered the Hakka church in Kuangtung province a growing and "fairly self-contained" church. He estimated that within the German missions there were 21,000 Christians, of whom 14,000 were communicants, and that the entire Hakka Protestant community in Kuangtung province was 30,000.[18a]

HAKKA DICTIONARY, HAKKA BIBLE, AND HAKKA
CHRISTIAN LITERATURE

Hamberg of the Basel Mission was the first Westerner to learn the Hakka language. As soon as he arrived in Hong Kong, he started to compile a Hakka dictionary. After his death in 1854 in Hong Kong, the work was continued and completed by his colleague Lechler. This manuscript, partly Chinese-English and partly Chinese-German, was copied by all younger missionaries connected with the Basel and Berlin Missions. Then D. MacIver, the English Presbyterian missionary at Wukingfu, reedited the entire manuscript and had it published in Shanghai in 1905 as *An English-Chinese Dictionary in the Vernacular of the Hakka People in the Canton Province* in a thirteen-hundred-page volume.

Translation of a Hakka Bible was largely done by Basel missionaries. The gospel of Matthew, the first Bible portion in the Hakka language, was published by Basel Mission in 1860 in Roman script. In 1866 it was put out again by the British and Foreign Bible Society, with the gospel of Luke added. By 1883 the entire New Testament was available in Hakka in both Roman script and Chinese characters.[19]

In 1885 Charles Piton, also of the Basel Mission, standardized the system of writing Hakka language in Chinese characters so that the Roman script could gradually be displaced in all important publications. In 1916 the entire Old and New Testaments was published by British and Foreign Bible Society in Hakka in Chinese characters.[20]

In *The Bible in China,* Broomhall mentioned a Bible version in Wukingfu, which is a variation of the Hakka language prevailing in areas near Swatow.[20a]

In 1879 Edward H. Parker wrote an article entitled: "Syllabary of the Hakka Language or Dialect" which appeared in *China Review.*[21] In it he listed some seven hundred Hakka sounds. Later in 1909 MacIver published his one-hundred-ninety-page book, *A Hakka Syllabary,* in Shanghai.

In the 1880s James Dyer Ball published two books in Hong Kong: *Easy Sentences in the Hakka Dialect,* and *Hakka Made Easy.*

Oehler[22] mentioned that the smaller and the greater catechism, liturgy, Bible history, collection of sermons, hymns, church papers, and tracts had been made available in Hakka.

ROMAN CATHOLIC WORK AMONG THE HAKKAS

In seeking to understand the situation of church growth in a certain area, it is usually enlightening to compare the work of the Protestant missionaries with that of the Roman Catholics.

A HAKKA CONVERT MADE THE START

The Roman Catholic church in the Hakka areas in Kuangtung Province was begun in 1850 at the request of a Hakka man returning from Malaya, where he had been converted. The following account was taken from the diary of Père Hervel of the Paris Foreign Mission Society:

> A young man named Hung-Tong had gone to Siam and thence to Penang to seek his fortune. There he heard about the Christian doctrine. He believed and embraced the religion of the Lord of Heaven in 1844. Returning to his native village of Shou-Hang, about fifteen miles from Kaying, he brought the faith to some of his relatives. Hung-Tong continued his

efforts to win others to Christ and in a few years he had many believers around him who asked [Bishop of Canton] for a priest to come and baptize them. Their desire was soon fulfilled. Father Le Turdu . . . came to Kaying early in 1850.[23]

The French priests continued to labor among the Hakkas there, but persecution was so strong that no progress could be made. And

> in 1851, the Christians of Shou-Hang were falsely accused of crimes against the State and soldiers were sent to burn the little chapel and to arrest Father Le Turdu . . . . The Hakka Christians suffered continually during those early years. Chapels were desecrated, Christian families were harassed, young men known to be Catholic were refused opportunities for political or educational advancement.[24]

After a strong protest from the French government in 1885, however, serious persecution stopped and the Hakka mission began to gain in the number of converts.

THE HAKKA MISSION

The work in the Hakka territory became too big for the missionaries of the Paris Foreign Mission Society in the Swatow vicariate to carry. Therefore in 1925 the Congregation for the Propagation of Faith decided to create a new mission in the Hakka area and assign it to the Maryknoll fathers who had already been working in or near Canton. A young Maryknoller, Francis Ford from New York, was sent to set up the new Kaying Mission, a Hakka mission indeed, which bordered the territory of German Dominican Fathers in Fukien, and that of American Vincentians in Kiangsi. The three and half million people in this area were scattered in seventy-eight market towns and numerous villages.[25]

When Ford took over the work from the French priests in 1925, there were ten parishes with thirty-seven small chapels, eleven elementary schools, and some four thousand Catholics. In the See city of Kaying, however, there were no "established chapels, schools, or residences for the missioners."[26]

The first few years of Ford's work was spent in consolidating the local churches so there was but a very slow increase in the number of Christians. However, Ford found the Hakkas very hospitable to him, and he had great hope for them.[27]

Contrary to the beliefs of his European colleagues, Ford strongly believed in building up a Chinese priesthood. No sooner had he arrived in the new field than he invited eight Hakka boys to live with him for the purpose of training. During the first years, much of his effort was placed in establishing the local seminary.[28]

In 1928 the Kaying mission, already reinforced with two Chinese priests and seven Maryknollers, was made a "prefecture," and Ford was nominated its prefect apostolic with the title monsignor. In 1935 Kaying prefecture was further promoted to a vicariate, and Ford became its first bishop.[29]

In the 1930s Ford placed great emphasis on evangelism. Under him, missionaries all had to do direct evangelism among unbelievers. Maryknoll sisters were invited to work among women. Believers were trained to participate in spreading the faith. As a result, membership increased steadily. By 1940 there were about twenty thousand Catholics.[30]

It is apparent from the preceding accounts that both the Protestant and the Roman Catholic churches among the Hakkas on mainland China have grown just as well as if not better than the church among the other peoples in China. But, could it be that the Hakkas in Taiwan are more resistant than their kinsmen on the mainland? It hardly seems so. Usually migrated people are more open to accepting new ideas. In this connection, a glance at the growth of the Roman Catholic Church in Taiwan is most revealing.

THE FASTEST GROWING ROMAN CATHOLIC DIOCESE IN TAIWAN

In Taiwan, a startling fact is: the Roman Catholic diocese of Hsinchu (covering the three predominantly Hakka counties of Taoyuan, Hsinchu, and Miaoli) is the *fastest-growing diocese on the whole island,* gaining 26,910 in membership in five years, as shown in table 4.

Allowing for the different standards with which the

Protestants and Roman Catholics count their membership, the growth of the Catholic church in Hsinchu diocese is still amazing. Although Hualien diocese also enjoyed a large gain during the same period of time; its gain has come mainly from the accession of the Highlanders who constitute 30.7 percent of the population within Hualien diocese. In Hsinchu diocese, however, the Highlanders are only 1.8 percent of the population; therefore the remarkable increase (26,910) must have been partly from the Hakkas. What a contrast this is to the tiny Hsinchu presbytery in the same geographical area! Especially when we remember that the Presbyterians were there long before the Roman Catholics.

ROMAN CATHOLIC WORK IN TAIWAN

After a period of pioneering work during 1626-1643, Dominican missionaries reentered Taiwan in 1859. Their work was centered at Kaohsiung and developed gradually northward. Due to severe persecution, progress was very slow. The number of the Catholic community was 1,300 in 1895; 3,000 in 1913; and 8,000 in 1945.[31]

Growth began to accelerate when a large number of missionaries and large material resources were sent to Taiwan from mainland China during the early 1950s. Many Catholics came over with the immigrants from the mainland. Many Highlanders, Mainlanders, and some Taiwanese became Catholics. By 1959 their number in Taiwan had increased to 163,463.[32] In 1966 community membership reached 293,446.[33]

The Diocese of Hsinchu was established in 1961 to cover the three counties of Taoyuan, Hsinchu, and Miaoli, where almost all Hakka people in the north are included. Most of the churches in this diocese, however, were started late— that is, during the years 1953-1959. In the 1967 *Catholic Directory*, the year of beginning of the churches is listed. See table 5, page 37.

CATHOLIC MEMBERSHIP

After the peak years of church-founding were over, the membership figure continued to climb. This can be seen from the statistics for Hsinchu diocese, given in table 4.

TABLE 4

ROMAN CATHOLIC MEMBERSHIP IN TAIWAN

Diocese	1961	1962	1963	1964	1965	1966	Increase Between 1961-66
Taipei	32,982	34,992	38,075	41,145	43,165	44,420	11,438
Hsinchu	34,667	41,104	47,184	53,823	58,252	61,577	26,910
Taichung	30,021	32,934	35,919	38,309	39,850	41,167	11,146
Chiayi	12,069	14,186	16,435	17,562	19,384	20,283	8,214
Tainan	15,000	17,000	19,108	21,025	21,988	21,503	6,503
Kaohsiung	36,751	38,725	42,040	44,406	46,423	47,831	11,080
Hualien	37,559	41,560	46,053	49,285	54,012	56,665	19,106
Total	199,049	220,501	244,814	265,555	283,074	293,446	94,397

SOURCE: Data from *Catholic Directory of Taiwan, 1967*, p. 374.

TABLE 5

ROMAN CATHOLIC CHURCHES IN HSINCHU DIOCESE

Year of Beginning	Number of Churches in Predominantly Hakka Areas	Number of Churches in Non-Hakka Areas
1952	1	2
1953	11	2
1954	8	2
1955	2	12
1956	5	9
1957	2	1
1958	4	1
1959	2	1
1960		
1961	1	1
1962		1
1963	2	
1964		3
1965		1
Totals	38	36

It is difficult, however, to ascertain the exact number of Hakka congregations or Hakka members in the overall statistics, as ethnic distinction is usually not made. Nor is it safe to estimate Hakka membership by counting the number of chapel buildings in Hakka areas. In the Catholic work, buildings often exist before there are congregations of comparable size, and the congregations may or may not be Hakka. Nevertheless, in the following paragraphs, we shall attempt to estimate the size of Hakka segments contained in the membership figures of Hsinchu diocese (61,577) and Kaohsiung diocese (47,831).

In the 1967 *Catholic Directory,* some 108 congregations are listed under Hsinchu diocese. About fifty-six churches and chapels are in predominantly Hakka areas. In the south, the Hakka population comes under Kaohsiung diocese which covers Kaohsiung and Pingtung counties. We count nine in Hakka areas. These make a total of sixty-five presumably Hakka congregations, which is about one-tenth of the total of some 650 congregations listed for the whole island.

If we take the average size of a Hakka congregation as being equal to the island-wide average size, the number of Hakka Catholics should be also one-tenth of the total membership, or 29,000, which is about six times the size of the Protestant Hakka community. Even if we take the size of an average Hakka congregation to be only one-third of the overall average size, as we find in the case of Hakka Protestants, there would still be at least some 10,000 Hakka Catholics—twice as many as Hakka Protestants.

HAKKAS MAKE GOOD CHRISTIANS

Finally, another evidence favorable to the Hakkas can be found within the Protestant church itself. In Taiwan, the Hakka church may be small, but it has produced some of the best Christian leaders. In the Taipei urban area, the pastors of three of the large Presbyterian (Minnan) churches are Hakkas. One of them was the education and youth secretary of the general assembly. Another has held leadership positions on the presbytery, synod, and general assembly levels.

Under the missionary program of Taiwan Presbyterian church, eight pastors have been sent to overseas Chinese churches as missionaries, and four of them are Hakkas.

In the interviews which the writer had with Taiwan pastors, a great many, including the evangelism secretary of the Presbyterian general assembly, testified that the Hakka people, once converted, became staunch Christians not likely to revert.

In the face of such evidences of responsiveness, how can we account for the retarded growth of the Hakka Protestant church in Taiwan? Why is it that many tend to think the Hakkas are resistant? To understand the problem more thoroughly, we will look into the history of the Hakka church in Taiwan.

4

A FALTERING GROWTH

ARE THE HAKKAS in Taiwan resistant? Or, are they not? From the very beginning of modern missionary activities in Taiwan, the Hakkas have had their opportunities to hear the gospel. If they are not resistant, why is it that the church among them is so small? Could it not be that the meager growth proves their resistance?

To answer such questions, one must look more deeply into the history of the church. Lack of growth may indicate resistance, but it may also indicate neglect. A historical study will help us to understand correctly the situation of "resistant" peoples, and to formulate more effective policies for winning them to Christ.

SOUTHERN TAIWAN

THE BEGINNING BY THE ENGLISH PRESBYTERIAN MISSION (1865–1897)

In 1865, two centuries after Dutch missionaries were expelled from Taiwan, the modern era of Protestant work began with the arrival of Dr. James Maxwell, medical missionary of the English Presbyterian Mission. He chose Tainan, the prefectural city, as the center of his work, although for the first three years, because of severe persecution, he had to make his headquarters at Takao, the treaty port thirty miles to the south, now called Kaohsiung.

In 1867 Maxwell was joined by the Reverend Hugh Ritchie, the first ordained missionary to arrive in Taiwan. Later in 1871 and 1875 respectively, the Reverend William Campbell and the Reverend Thomas Barclay came to strengthen the force. These pioneers itinerated frequently and widely in the surrounding villages and towns, giving medical service, distributing tracts, and preaching the gospel.

EARLY HAKKA CONVERTS

By 1872 seven churches had been established. One was located in a village called Taw-kun-eng (in Nei-p'u township, Pingtung county), where the Hakkas were found in villages scattered among the Minnan-speaking population. A talented man, Ritchie also learned the Hakka language in addition to Minnan, so before long a number of Hakka converts were joining the congregation at Taw-kun-eng. But because of the inconvenience involved in traveling to Minnan villages (where the church buildings were) as well as in the pain of worshiping in the Minnan language, the Hakka Christians decided to form a congregation of their own.

They had great difficulty, however, in securing a property in any Hakka village for a church building, as the conservative clan leaders had banded together against it. At one time the building materials prepared by the Christians were stolen overnight. Finally a Hakka Christian—Tiu A-kim—and his wife offered their own house at Ji-lun to be the meeting place, and it was in this Hakka village that an unforgettable episode happened to missionary Thomas Barclay. It greatly strengthened the faith of those first Hakka Christians and laid a foundation for the first Hakka church in that area.

MISSIONARY BRAVES NIGHTSOIL TREATMENT, (1885)

A vivid description of this incident, given by Barclay himself, was quoted by his fellow missionary Edward Band in his book *Barclay of Formosa:*

> In June 1885 a meeting of the brethren took place [at Ji-lun] at which they were attacked and very roughly handled by the people of the village. They sent messengers to the city to inform us, and I was appointed to go down and see what could be done. I arrived on Saturday 18th July, and that

evening had two meetings with the elders of the village (not the church elders but the chief men of the village). They were unable to contest our right to the site, but feared that there would be a serious disturbance if a meeting took place. The young men of the village, they said, were very much opposed to the church and might take violent steps which the elders would not be able to control. We resolved, however, on holding our meeting, and on Sunday morning some twenty or thirty of the brethren met with me for service. Whilst we were still engaged in worship we heard the beating of a gong and the word was passed round, "They are coming!"

The little room in which we met opened directly into the open air, and we saw them enter into the court-yard, bearing—I am almost ashamed to write it—several loads of filth gathered from the village dunghills. We at once closed the doors and got into the corners of the room. But the doors were soon broken to pieces by stones, and then they ladled in filth till the room was all polluted and some of us splashed. Then I stepped out in front to tell them that we yielded to superior force, and would not meet again till the authorities had been consulted. But they refused to listen, and continued ladling filth upon me from head to foot. I soon saw enough to convince me that they had been carefully instructed not to injure the foreigner, so I simply stood still and let them go on pouring the manure over me as long as they chose; which had the further good effect of amusing the crowd looking on, and that was a point in our favour.

When the incident is narrated (and sometimes acted out) by the Formosan Christians, it is reported of me—though I have no memory of it myself—as an illustration of my goodness of heart, that when they were ladling out the filth all over me, I remonstrated with them saying, "What a waste of good manure! You will need this when you are planting out the rice!" I imagine if I did say anything of the kind, it was more by way of chaffing them than out of goodness of heart.

Some of our assailants however became all the more enraged. They dragged out by the hair of the head or any way, the unresisting Christians, plucked out their beards, tore off their clothes and beat them till I saw the marks of the blows rising on their backs. I did what I could to intercede for them but it only made the mob more angry at myself. They cursed me, and, carried away with passion, raised their sticks to beat me but had their hands stayed by others more cautious. They made special search for the owner of the house, beating in the walls of the rooms looking for him. Fortunately he had gone elsewhere for the day, or he might have lost his life. Then when their work was done they went off leaving a large crowd to look at me drenched with filth from tip to toe. All the congregation had scattered, but some women and some heathen members of the household attended to me. I got a bath and, having no change of clothing, put on my sleeping suit and had some dinner. I remained on, instead of returning to Taw-kun-eng, in order to let them know that we did not abandon our claim to the building . . . .

Later on a woman from Taw-kun-eng brought me a letter from the brethren there, warning me against staying the night in Ji-lun, as there was danger of an attack being made, and advised me to come away with the woman, who would carry my burden for me. I packed up a few things and went with her . . . .

Some days later on returning to Taiwanfu [Tainan] I found that my servant had come back in haste from Ji-lun and given to the missionaries an exaggerated account of what had taken place, and they had already sent in a statement to the Consul, who brought the matter before the Governor. The latter, I am told, was very indignant, and sent down a special commissioner to assist the magistrate at Pi-thau in managing the case. These two officials went to Ji-lun to investigate, but met with such a rough reception that they were obliged to return without effecting anything. The Governor informed the Consul that it would be impossible to make any arrests without calling out the military, which the Consul declared, and we agreed with him, would be undesirable. Ultimately the case was settled by one or two men being arrested and beaten.[1]

Band added:

The Formosan Christians have never forgotten this incident. It is frequently recited in praise of Barclay's meek and forbearing Christian spirit. Moreover they do not fail to appreciate the Scotch humour of his reply to his assailants. Where could a more appropriate illustration be found of the text: "Being reviled, we bless; being persecuted, we endure; being defamed, we intreat: We are made as the filth of the world, the offscouring of all things"?[2]

AN OSTRACIZED FAMILY

Tiu A-kim, the owner of the house, also came to Tainan to give a report, where he died unexpectedly of an epidemic in a few days. His wife was driven out by the Ji-lun villagers, and the house confiscated by the clan. Mrs. Tiu, still holding fast to her faith, went to nearby villages to live as a servant. She took with her the only close relative, Tiu An-kui, an eleven-year-old son of her husband's brother. An-kui was put through the mission school and seminary by Barclay, and later became a pastor. He married a Minnan wife and worked in Minnan areas. His son Tiu Sun-un, also a pastor, returned in 1932 to the Hakka area to minister to the only Hakka church at Nei-p'u, in a language he had to learn all over again.

In an interview with the writer, the Reverend Tiu Sun-un, now retired, reminisced over the early story which he heard from his father Tiu An-kui. While studying at the mission boarding school, An-kui used to make visits to his aunt at somebody else's home. When it was time for them to part, the dear lady would accompany the boy out of the village, and there on the gravelly shore by the river, the two lone souls would kneel down and pray. God alone was their solace, God alone knows what a price they had paid in order to be faithful to Him.

THE FIRST HAKKA CHURCH (1897)

The Hakka Christians were not discouraged in their desire to build their own church, and the matter was expedited by a flood in 1896 which wiped out the village of Taw-kun-eng. The church there was moved farther away from Hakka villages. Finally the Hakka brethren managed to build a chapel in an out-of-the-way Hakka village called Yu-liao, and the first Hakka church came into being in 1897. In 1927 it was moved to the market town of Nei-p'u, and renamed Nei-p'u church. Aside from a preaching center in the nearby village Wan-man which the Hakka Christians at Nei-p'u opened and maintained during the years 1931—1940, Nei-p'u church remained *the only Hakka congregation in southern Taiwan until 1951.*

NEW BURDEN AND NEW FRUIT (1947–1962)

With the termination of the war in 1945, Christians in Taiwan began to enjoy complete religious freedom under the Chinese constitution. A God-given spirit of revival brought the church to look ahead with new hope. In 1947, Hakka Christians gathered at Nei-p'u church to celebrate its jubilee, and a new burden was placed in the hearts of all those participating in the meeting: We must reach out for more Hakka souls!

Between 1951 and 1962, nine new congregations were established in the major Hakka areas in the south. Serving as the headquarters of the Hakka work was a "Hakka Evangelism Department," established in 1951 under Kaosiung Presbytery (covering Kaohsiung and Pingtung counties). The department started immediately to ask the youth groups in the Presbyterian churches all over the island to save NT$0.50 (US$0.0125) per person per month to help build new Hakka chapels.

The first two new Hakka congregations were established at Chu-t'ien and Wan-man, both in the vicinity of Nei-p'u. There were already Christians living in these two villages. Chu-t'ien is next to Ji-lun village where Barclay was insulted, and Wan-man had a chapel during 1931-1940. So both these congregations were merely productive divisions from Nei-p'u, and only these two later grew into fully self-supporting status.

The congregations at Chia-tung, Hsin-pei, and Lun-shang, were formed through similar process—by productive divisions of Hakka Christians from existing Minnan congregations, although they all grew by receiving some new converts. In the early fifties, Dr. George Hudson of the Presbyterian U.S. Mission responded to the invitation of the presbytery and came down to hold tent mettings at Chia-tung and Hsin-pei, one month in each place, and to channel gifts of US$1,000 each to these two new congregations to help in the church building funds.

The remaining three new congregations (Mei-nung, San-lin, and Hsi-shih) were largely the result of pioneering evangelism. The Reverend Fang Kuang-sheng, a Hakka pastor who wrote a series of articles in the *Presbyterian*

Church Bulletin in 1952 to appeal strongly for the one hundred seventy thousand Hakka souls then living in southern Taiwan, made a seventy-six-day evangelistic tour throughout eighteen Hakka villages in the same year. In 1954 he took up residence at Mei-nung, a very conservative Hakka town with a population of about forty thousand, and set up a chapel there. Miss Jessie Ammonds of Overseas Missionary Fellowship (formerly China Inland Mission) volunteered at that time to do Hakka work with the Presbyterian church, and was sent to San-lin to open a chapel among the Hakka farmers up in the mountains in Kaohsiung county. Hsi-shih chapel, pioneered by the "Hakka Evangelism Department," was the last and weakest among the new congregations. As a matter of fact, it is now practically closed down.

NORTHERN TAIWAN

THE BEGINNING BY THE CANADIAN PRESBYTERIAN MISSION (1872–1901)

Whereas southern Taiwan was jointly pioneered by several missionaries, the work in the north for the first three decades was largely through the effort and leadership of one man. Dr. George MacKay was sent by Canadian Presbyterian Mission to Taiwan in 1872. Upon arrival at Takao, he was guest of the Reverend Hugh Ritchie who later accompanied him to Tamsui, the northern treaty port, to start his pioneering work.

Laboring alone, MacKay set up a preaching room at Tamsui, but also it inerated widely. Preaching, tract distributing, and medical service (especially tooth-extracting) constituted his daily work. Before long, God gave the fruit, and MacKay was able to teach the truth to the first few converts and give them on-the-job training by taking them along in preaching tours. By the time he went back to Canada with his Taiwanese wife for the first furlough in 1880 (after nine years), he had seen twenty congregations, mostly Minnan-speaking, established in northern Taiwan.

But Mackay also had early contact with the Hakkas. Hsinchu, sixty miles southwest of Taipei, is the largest city among Hakka settlements in the north. Being a business town, however, the main bulk of its population is Minnan. In his book *From Far Formosa*. MacKay wrote about how the Hsinchu church was established in 1878:

> Tek-chham [Hsinchu], a walled city of forty thousand inhabitants, was one of the places visited on my first trip down the west coast the week after landing at Tamsui in 1872. I had a "prophet's chamber" there, and after frequent visits succeeded in renting a small house for chapel purposes. No sooner had we got the place cleaned out than indignant crowds filled the narrow street, jostling, reviling, spitting in our faces. After three days the turmoil ceased, largely through the influence of a literary man to whom I had given medicine on a previous occasion. Within a month thirty persons enrolled themselves as Christians, and larger premises had to be secured. The work grew until still larger building was required. There is now a large preaching hall, with real glass in the front windows; and there a once proud Confucianist graduate is preaching the Gospel of Christ.[3]

Besides the Hsinchu church which is but partly Hakka, three other Hakka churches that exist today had their beginning during MacKay's days. They are Miaoli, Kung-kuan, and Chung-li.

In 1890, three believers from Miaoli, a large Hakka city, went up to see MacKay and ask him to start a chapel in their town. Believers were added, and the church grew so well that in 1899 some members living in the neighboring market town Kung-kuan started their own chapel. Another congregation was also formed in 1891 in Chung-li, a large Hakka town on the main highway and railroad between Taipei and Hsinchu. It also grew well, and later, after World War II, became the mother of no less than five more Hakka congregations in the vicinity.

SECOND PERIOD OF CHURCH GROWTH (1910–1926)

MacKay died in 1901 in Taiwan. With his death ended an era of missionary pioneering. But he had left behind him local disciples to carry on the work. The years 1910 through 1926 seemed to be a period of fervent evangelism and church planting undertaken by several Hakka preachers on fire for the Lord, the best known one being Chung A-mei. As a result of their zealous labor, six new Hakka congregations came into being. One was in the market town of Lung-t'an in Taoyuan county. Three were in Hsinchu county—Hsin-p'u, a market town, and Chu-tung and Kuan-hsi, two important commercial and industrial towns. The fifth one was in the inland market town of Nan-chuan in Miaoli county where the Hakka area borders the Highland territory. Another one was in Tung-shih, a business town in Taichung county at the southern edge of Hakkaland. These six congregations have all continued until today, although the Tung-shih church was reduced temporarily to a family meeting during World War II.

THIRD PERIOD OF CHURCH GROWTH (1952–1958)

As in the case of southern Taiwan, a high spirit of expectancy permeated the postwar Christians in the north. Chung-li church branched out in 1952, and in six years, five new congregations were formed in the vicinity. They are Hsin-wu, Yang-mei, P'u-hsin, Fu-kang, and Kuan-yin. The first-named two became organized churches. Fu-kang was later closed down.

The Hakka work in the north also received help from the presbytery. Funds collected from young people's saving accounts were dedicated to the building of new chapels. Help also came from the Presbyterian Bible School which was established in Taipei in 1952, but moved to Hsinchu area in 1955. The principal of the Bible school made it a routine to take students out to *preach and set up new congregations.* In 1956 two Hakka chapels—T'ou-feng and Hu-k'ou—were added in the vicinity of Hsinchu city. Hu-k'ou grew into an organized church in a few years.

Meanwhile, the church in Miaoli was forming branches in three neighboring small towns in Miaoli county—T'ung-lo, San-yi, and Hsing-lung—during 1954 through 1958. Farther southward, the Reverend William Junkin of the Presbyterian U.S. Mission was instrumental in building the family meeting in Tung-shih back up to a regular congregation in 1955, and in opening up a new one at Choh-lan at the same time.

So as a result of the efforts of God's people in the 1950s, three Hakka churches and seven Hakka chapels came into existence. Since 1958, however, none has been added.

HAKKA CHURCHES TODAY

So far discussion has been limited to the Presbyterian church. Now we want to examine briefly church multiplication among the Hakkas done by other missions. Most of them entered Taiwan during the early 1950s following the loss of the China mainland to the Communists. With years of experience on the mainland, it was natural for them to engage in missionary work among the spiritually hungry Mainlanders. As the years went by, however, their attention has shifted more and more to the local people.

The Swedish Holiness Mission settled in Hsinchu in the north. Its first Hakka chapels were started in 1958 in O-mei and Pei-p'u. Pei-p'u is now an organized self-supporting church. Out of the mission's seventeen congregations, nine are Hakka-speaking. The mission has two Hakka-speaking missionaries and four Hakka ministers, and is making preparations to begin more Hakka churches.

The Free Methodist Mission, located in the south, started a Hakka congregation in 1958 at the earnest request of a young Chinese couple burdened for the Hakka souls in Pingtung county. Scores of young converts were made at the initial preaching meetings, and some young people came to the mission's Bible school in Kaohsiung city for a short-term training. But because of the opposition from their families, these young converts never formed a church that could continue to grow.[4] The Free Methodist Mission now has two Hakka preachers in charge of three Hakka congregations (in Pingtung county) which constitute only a small part of the mission's forty-five congregations.

The Finnish Free Foreign Mission made Miaoli county its area of ministry; therefore, it naturally took up Hakka work in addition to the original Mandarin work. It now has thirteen Hakka congregations—all in Miaoli county except the one at Tung-shih, Taichung county.

In the following table are listed the number and membership of all Hakka congregations on the island. It must be pointed out, however, that the figures given here, as well as all other figures concerning Hakka Christians appearing elsewhere in this book, refer *only* to the Hakka Christians in predominantly Hakka congregations located in

TABLE 6
PROTESTANT HAKKA CONGREGATIONS IN TAIWAN
(1968)

DENOMINATIONS	Number of Hakka Congregations	Hakka Communicant * Membership	Hakka Christian Community†
Taiwan Presbyterian Church	30	1,224	2,800
True Jesus Church ‡	3	420	
Finnish Free Foreign Mission	13	137	
Swedish Holiness Mission	9	96	
Southern Baptist Mission	3	68	
Lutheran Brethren Mission	4	65	
Reformed Church	1	33	
Free Methodist Mission	3	26	1,800
Liebenzeller Mission	1	21	
Assembly of God	1	20	
The Evangelical Alliance Mission	1	15	
Norwegian Pentecostal	1	10	
Nazarene Mission	1	7	
Total	71 §	2,142	4,600

SOURCE: Field survey questionnaires returned by the churches, checked by information obtained from various mission headquarters.

* Only Hakka Members are counted. A minority of non-Hakkas usually exists in Hakka congregations.

† Community figure is obtained by doubling the communicant figure, except in the case of the Presbyterian church where the community/communicant ratio is known to be 2.3.

‡ Estimated by the writer.

§ The total number of Protestant congregations in Taiwan is 1,970 (*Taiwan Christian Yearbook 1968,* p. 158).

predominantly Hakka areas. There are other Hakka Christians who live in the rural frontiers on the east coast or in the large urban centers. In such places, the population is not predominantly Hakka and no Hakka church is in existence. These Hakka Christians join Minnan or Mandarin churches, and their number is not included in what is termed "Hakka Christian" in our present study. It is worth noting that the average Hakka congregation numbers thirty full members only. The Hakka church consists of about seventy very small churches widely scattered in a dozen denominational and geographical pockets.

Early Hakka Congregations That Have
Ceased to Exist

The history of the Hakka church in Taiwan as outlined in the foregoing sections is only part of the story. By itself, it does not tell much about how responsive or how resistant the Hakkas have been. But when one goes through the history of the missionary activities in Taiwan, it is most interesting to uncover, over and again, records of Hakka congregations that no longer exist today. These extinct Hakka churches seem to point to a period of responsiveness of the Hakkas—a responsiveness that could well have been greater than that of the Minnans.

Shortly after MacKay established the church in Hsinchu during his early years in Taiwan, he was invited to preach the gospel in a nearby Hakka village. He wrote:

> Ten miles from Tek-chham [Hsinchu], toward the mountains, is a Hakka village called Geh-bai. To this village we were led by several Hakkas who attended services in the city church. The villagers assembled under a beautiful banyan-tree, where fully a thousand people could find shelter from the broiling sun. They were greatly delighted, and one fine old gentleman welcomed us to his house for the night, one of the largest and cleanest in the island. The old man was genuinely interested, and walked many times to Tak-chham to the Sabbath services there. A great crowd gathered in the open court to hear the new doctrine that evening.[5]

The gospel was so earnestly received that an active congregation was immediately formed. MacKay wrote in the same paragraph:

> One man, seventy years of age, exerted himself with such success that a house was rented, repaired, and fitted up for chapel services. The congregation became organized and when a native preacher was sent among them four months of his salary was paid in advance. There in that Hakka village, high among the hills, is a flourishing, self-helping Christian congregation.[6]

Little further information, however, can be found about this once thriving church. Today in Geh-bai (O-mei) there is no Presbyterian church, although some Christians or Christian descendants still live there. Somehow the church died in its infancy.

A TRIP IN HAKKA HILLS

We also find an interesting account in MacKay's book about an inland tour he made in 1890 in Hakka territories:

> Sometimes we take . . . the less frequented paths inland from the sea, where the Chinese pioneers are subduing nature's wildness and opening the way for the advancing settlements. In 1890 we traversed the entire length of the field from north to south without once approaching the public road. The narrow paths along which we went skirted and climbed the rugged mountains and wound through scenery of extraordinary beauty.[7]

Then he told how on this trip he was guided by an old hillman (by which he meant Hakka, not Highlander) who "spoke a great deal about the folly of idolatry, and offered me his god of the north pole, god of the kitchen, and god of war, before which he had been bowing himself for seventy long years. This offer was made good, and on our return we carried them with us as a contribution to my museum at Tamsui."

That day the guide took MacKay to a schoolroom operated by a Confucian scholar who was widely respected around that area. The teacher had been given an Old Testament and a hymnbook by a native preacher, so he welcomed MacKay and his party very warmly. After MacKay's preaching at a nearby chapel that night, the Confucian stood up and openly declared himself "a believer in God and in Jesus" as he had known them from the Bible.

The next stop of their trip was Toa-kho-ham where Chinese camphor-workers (mostly Hakkas) were living. Following that, MacKay described another chapel meeting in that mountainous area:

> Our next night was spent at a village of Hakka Chinese . . . .
> At a chapel among the hillmen we were given a reception that, whatever might be said of its style, lacked nothing in the matter of heartiness. Guns and fire-crackers sounded out

their glad welcome. A sumptuous feast of fowl and fish was prepared at the chapel, and the building was filled the entire day. Three hours were spent in listening to their recitations of psalms, hymns, and Bible selections, some in the Hakka dialect and others in the Hoklo. Away yonder among the rugged hills a beacon-light is glowing, and those weary pioneers are finding their way back to God.[8]

Today we cannot locate this Hakka chapel either. It has vanished.

OTHER VANISHING CHURCHES

MacKay also worked in other Hakka places during his early years. In Hsu's *Centennial History*,[9] where each of the first twenty churches in the north is mentioned and briefly described, there is a church established in 1879 at Shih-tan, an inland Hakka village in Miaoli county. Today in this village there is no Presbyterian church, only some Christians meeting in families.

The writer was told that MacKay established at least two other congregations—one in Hsinchu county, near Hu-k'ou; another in Miaoli county, at Tou-huan-p'ing. These congregations have also vanished.

After MacKay's death in 1901, church-planting work still continued on, as we read from the writing of a Canadian missionary—Duncan MacLeod—that "In the spring of 1906, six new out-stations were opened, some of which were among the Hakka people."[10] But today, we can find no Hakka church that was established in that year.

The church-planting work carried out by Hakka pastors during the 1920s was quite fruitful, but the four Hakka congregations they planted have ceased to exist. Two were located in Hsinchu county, at Pei-p'u and Chun-lin, and two in Miaoli county, at Ta-hu and Nan-hu.

EARLY ACCESSION OF HAKKAS IN SOUTHERN TAIWAN

In southern Taiwan, similar cases can be found. Amidst persecutions caused by conservative Hakka villagers, the early missionaries also found encouraging signs of responsiveness. The Nei-p'u church mentioned earlier in this chapter was really not the first Hakka church in the south. In one of his outstanding books, *Missionary Success in the Island of Formosa*, English Presbyterian missionary William Campbell mentioned that Hugh Ritchie began to preach to the Hakkas in the early 1870s.[11] The first Hakka chapel was set up at Lam-gan (Nan-an, in Pingtung county). People were receptive. "We have now a prosperous little congregation there, and the worshippers who attend from other Hakka villages will no doubt use their influence in our favor when the time comes for further extension." In fact, it was the favorable situation at Lam-gan that prompted Ritchie to begin immediately the study of the Hakka language. Campbell also wrote about the impression he himself received during a personal visit to Lam-gan. "The chapel was uncomfortably crowded at both forenoon and afternoon times of worship . . . . I feel exceedingly thankful to say that the work here still points in the same encouraging direction."[12] After mentioning the continual increase of the number at Sunday worship, Campbell continued: "Lam-gan is one of our few stations at which there seems to be something really hopeful about the children's week-day school."[13] On that Sunday Campbell examined ten candidates for baptism. Seven were accepted.

Campbell also mentioned in his book a colporteur Pa and how this man worked among the Hakkas:

> On 14th May he went to the thriving town of Tang-si-kak [Tung-shih] where, among the intelligent Hakka population, he says, "God set before me an open door, and enabled me to speak the truth with a warm heart." One hundred and nineteen little pamphlets were sold in this place, 54 of these being purchased by a well-to-do man for distribution among his friends and neighbors. An old native doctor, the sign of whose shop is "Golden Longevity," was particularly pleased to listen to all that was said, and showed no small kindness to the preacher.[14]

In his *Centennial History,* Hsu mentioned a "Chien-kung-chuan church" existing in 1896 as one of the twenty-three organized churches forming the presbytery of Southern Taiwan.[15] The location is near the present-day Hsin-pei church established in the 1950s. The writer was told by a Hakka pastor that this early church was planted by William

Campbell and had some seventy Hakka believers and even a Hakka preacher. During a visit in 1968 to the present-day Hsin-pei church, located in a Hakka village, the writer saw an old membership roll carrying an entry of a lady baptized in 1874 by Campbell. But somehow the entire church has disappeared.

Also, in the August 1957 issue of the *Presbyterian Church Bulletin*, a speaker at the opening ceremony of the new Chia-tung church in that same area was quoted to have said that there were Christians around there some forty years ago, but since the church ceased to exist, the believers and their descendants backslid and even removed the cross from their family tombs. There was certainly a period of accession among the Hakkas in the south during the days of the early missionaries, but somehow the fruit was not conserved except in that one church at Nei-p'u.

All evidences seem to indicate, therefore, that the Hakkas both in the north and in the south were once responsive.

What has smothered this early responsiveness? What has caused the prosperous Hakka churches to lose their dynamics, to stand still, and even to disappear? What rendered a growing church incapable even to retain its own second generation? The Hakkas certainly are not resistant. What, then, has happened to their church? Can they illustrate similar ethnic groups in Asia, Africa, and Latin America which look resistant but really are not?

5

NEGLECTED

LITTLE LABOR, TINY MANPOWER

To DISCOVER THE REASONS for a weak Hakka church in Taiwan, one does not have to go far. In answering the questions given in the survey conducted by the writer in 1968, many ministers pointed out the failure of the church in having systematic evangelization and church-planting programs specially directed to the Hakka area (see table 2). This can be clearly seen from the history of the church.

THE SHORT-LIVED "HAKKA EVANGELISM BOARD" (1958—1965)

Despite the appeal voiced by zealous Hakka ministers and Christians, the Presbyterian church has made no continuing efforts to win the Hakkas. The only gesture toward Hakka evangelization was the "Hakka Evangelism Board" formed in 1958 under the general assembly—a mere enlargement of the one already in existence under Kaohsiung presbytery in the south. Plans were made to push Hakka evangelization through such means as evangelistic teams, radio, conferences, and promotion of Hakka Christian literature in Roman script. But little was actually accomplished. Between 1958 and 1965 the expenditures of the Hakka Evangelism Board, as the writer found in the minutes of the general assemblies, were as follows:

1958	NT$ 11,046.80	(US$ 276)
1959	NT$ 9,656.60	(US$ 241)
1960	not indicated	
1961	not indicated	

1962	not indicated	
1963	NT$ 50,535.10	(US$ 1,263)
1964	NT$ 20,685.20	(US$ 517)
1965	no budget allocated	

The annual budgeted income for the board was a subsidy of NT$ 27,000 (US$ 675)—and stopped in 1965. In the 1966 general assembly, the Hakka Evangelism Board was voted out of existence on the ground that it could not present a work report. Apparently there was some internal tension. To remedy the feelings, however, the 1968 general assembly adopted a resolution, on the recommendation of twelve pastors, to establish a "Hakka Evangelism Sub-committee" under the evangelism committee of the general assembly. In view of the present indifference of the church, it remains to be seen how much this subcommittee can accomplish.

LACK OF PRESBYTERIAN MISSIONARIES FOR THE HAKKAS

Throughout the entire century of Protestant missions in Taiwan, the Hakkas have never had a quota of missionaries especially assigned to them. A few missionaries, however, did see the need of doing evangelistic work in the Hakka language. Back in the 1860s, Ritchie began to learn Hakka and developed a good ministry in planting Hakka churches. His early death in 1879, after only twelve years of field work in Taiwan, was certainly a loss to the cause of Hakka evangelization. Nobody seemed to continue in his vision, as William Campbell wrote in 1915, thirty-six years later.

> We much regret that there is not yet any missionary in the Island who has learned the spoken language of the Hakkas. There is a fine opportunity for evangelistic work in that direction, and our fervent hope is that full advantage may be taken of it before long.[1]

In northern Taiwan, a similar situation existed. Writing about the Hakkas in Hsinchu area, Canadian Presbyterian missionary Duncan MacLeod said:

> There are eleven preaching stations among these people, but *they have never had a foreign missionary who could preach in their own dialect.* This district [Hsinchu] needs at least one

ordained missionary and two woman evangelists . . . . In the city [of Hsinchu] a fine plot of land has been bought, and a mission station is to be opened in the near future. Several missionaries should be located here to carry on the work among the Hakkas and the Hoklos of this extensive territory.[2]

Such an aggressive plan to reach the Hakkas was made in 1922 when the Presbyterian church of Northern Taiwan celebrated its jubilee. Appeal was made to add twenty-eight more missionaries to the field. But unfortunately this plan was never carried out, for in 1925, back in Canada, a division occurred in the Canadian Presbyterian Church, with one part joining the United Church and the other choosing to remain Presbyterian. Northern Taiwan field happened to be assigned to the new Presbyterian mission in 1927; and therefore the missionaries who were on the side of the United Church decided to leave. During the years 1927 to 1931, twenty missionaries left; only five remained. Especially affecting the Hakka work was the departure of MacLeod himself, who was

TABLE 7

HAKKA-SPEAKING MISSIONARIES

Missions	Doing Evangelistic Work	Teaching	Learning Language	Total
Overseas Missionary Fellowship	2	1		3
The Evangelical Alliance Mission	2			2
Swedish Holiness Mission	1		1	2
Finish Free Foreign Mission			1	1
Independent Pentecostal	1			1
Total	6	1	2	9

a strong advocate of Hakka evangelism but nevertheless chose to transfer himself to the southern Taiwan field in 1927. Since that time until 1952, a full quarter-century later, no new Hakka congregation was added.

According to the minutes of the Presbyterian general assembly in 1959, a request was made by Hakka churches for missionaries to be assigned to Hakka areas. The general assembly granted the request and resolved to pass it on to the personnel committee for execution. But in the general assembly in 1964, the same request was made by Hakka churches again. Apparently no action was taken. The only Hakka-speaking missionaries connected with the Presbyterian church during the past two decades were the two or three ladies on loan from Overseas Missionary Fellowship.

Down to the present moment, the need is still appalling. The number of Hakka-speaking foreign missionaries, as shown in table 7, was noted by the writer during the survey trips.

In *Taiwan Christian Yearbook 1968,* the total number of Protestant missionaries in Taiwan is listed as 849. Among them 106 are associated with Taiwan Presbyterian Church, but none of them is engaged in active Hakka work.

TABLE 8
MINISTERS OF HAKKA CONGREGATIONS

The Minister	Number of Hakka Presbyterian Congregations	Number of Hakka Congregations of Other Denominations	Total
A Hakka	17	17	34
Not a Hakka	11	16	27
Not indicated	2	8	10
Preaches in Hakka	17	21	38
Does not preach in Hakka	11	12	23
Not indicated	2	8	10

SHORTAGE OF MAN-POWER

In table 2 lack of Hakka-speaking church workers is the most frequently mentioned failure on the part of the church. The Hakka congregations are constantly in need of Hakka-speaking ministers. Several respondents mentioned that even Hakka ministers do not stay long in Hakka areas. Table 8, also compiled from Questionnaire A of the field survey (appendix D), shows the inadequate number of Hakka-speaking ministers who are serving in seventy-one Hakka congregations. Only thirty-four of them are Hakkas, and thirty-eight preach in the Hakka language.

Such a lack of personnel for the Hakkas testifies strongly to the neglect which causes the retarded growth of the Hakka church. This point is all the more convincing when we find out the Roman Catholic Church has assigned twenty percent of its priests and sisters to Hsinchu diocese, the predominantly Hakka areas, as shown in table 9.[3]

Having seen the meager effort put in Hakka areas by the Protestant church, the question that confronts us now is: Why has there been such a lack?

TABLE 9

ROMAN CATHOLIC PERSONNEL IN HSINCHU DIOCESE
(1966)

Location	Priests	Sisters	Total
Total in Taiwan	871 300 secular 190 Jesuit 381 of other orders	975	1,846
Number in Hsinchu Diocese	165 21 secular 82 Jesuit 62 of other orders	209	374 20% of total in Taiwan

THE ONE-LANGUAGE POLICY

Why did the Presbyterian missions fail to assign part of their personnel to the Hakka church, as was the practice of their colleagues on mainland China? (The English Presbyterian Mission that pioneered in southern Taiwan is the same mission that has established a Hakka mission center and a Hakka presbytery in Kuangtung province.) Why, again, has the Taiwan Presbyterian Church also failed to see the need of a specialized program, in terms both of organization and of training of workers, for the evangelization of the Hakkas? This continued lack of personnel and efforts does not seem incidental. Could it be a matter of policies?

Throughout the years, the Presbyterian church has evidently adopted a one-language policy. Minnan, the majority language among both Christians and non-Christians, has been made the one and only official language of the Presbyterian church. In the presbytery, the synod, the general assembly; in youth camps, conferences, councils; Minnan alone was spoken. (Only until very recently was a simultaneous translation into Mandarin provided in the general assembly meetings, and this for the convenience of the Highland delegates.) Christian literature was printed only in Minnan. Seminary students learned everything in Minnan. By and by, the difference in languages was brushed aside. The habit of one-language policy has even given rise to an extreme view that evangelizing the Hakkas in Minnan is the normal—and even the correct—thing to do. On a visit to a rural Hakka church, the writer asked the Minnan pastor why he still preached in Minnan since he could also speak good Hakka. He replied, "I have been requested by the Hakka Christians to do so, because *certain Christian tenets can be adequately expressed only in Minnan.*" This shows how little Christianity has been developed in the Hakka tongue. This same pastor expressed his disappointment over the fact that the Hakka Christians do not like to learn to read the Minnan Bible, and thus do not grow spiritually.

NO HAKKA BIBLE AND HAKKA HYMNAL

The complete lack of a Hakka Bible and Hakka hymnals, at least for the first century of the missionary work in

Taiwan, is almost unbelievable. It is the direct outcome of
the one-language policy. The writing system of the Hakka
language developed or standardized by missionaries on the
mainland, either in Roman script or in Chinese characters,
has not been utilized by the church in Taiwan. Years ago
Hakka Bibles and hymnals were introduced to Taiwan from
the English Presbyterian Mission on the mainland, but
somehow the use was not continued. One reason frequently
given is that the variety of the Hakka language used in the
mainland Christian literature is somewhat different from the
form prevalent in Taiwan. Whatever the reason, no lasting
effort was made to secure the kind of Bible and hymnals
which are suitable for use among Hakka Christians in
Taiwan. The Canadian missionary Duncan MacLeod did
advocate the use of Hakka in Roman script, but he soon left
northern Taiwan and no one seemed to carry on the task.
Therefore, throughout the years, the Hakka Christians in
Taiwan have been using Mandarin or Minnan Bibles and
hymnbooks in their worship.

Once in a while Hakka Christians voiced their desire for
improvement. In June 1952, an article by the Reverend Fang
Kuang-sheng, a fervent Hakka evangelist, appeared in the
Presbyterian Church Bulletin in which he expressed cordial
gratitude for the fact that the Bible had been translated by a
missionary into the Minnan language, so that the Hakkas, *by
learning Minnan*, can share in the blessings of the Christian
faith. He then tactfully reported that there was a committee
organized to study the writing system of Hakka in Roman
script, and already there were some one hundred fifteen
hymns translated into Hakka. Finally, he hoped a Hakka
Bible would soon appear.

It was not until about 1960 that the American Bible
Society took up the project of producing, in Roman script, a
new Hakka Bible. Fang Kuang-sheng was one of the four
translators appointed by the American Bible Society. The
manuscript for the entire New Testament has been finished,
and is scheduled to be published in 1970.

As to a Hakka hymnbook, so far as is known, the only one
now available in Taiwan is *The Hakka Hymnal* (1967) put out
by the Assembly of God. It contains one hundred fifty

conventional hymns translated into Hakka, and is available in both Roman script and Chinese characters.

Up to the present time, the Hakka churches have been using two versions of the Bible:

1. The Minnan Bible, available only in Roman script. This has to be read in Minnan. Only a few very skillful pastors can read Hakka directly from a Minnan Bible.

2. The Mandarin Bible, in Chinese characters. This can be read in Hakka with some extemporized modifications.

Table 10, compiled from survey Questionnaire A, shows the situation:

TABLE 10
VERSIONS OF BIBLE USED BY HAKKA CONGREGATIONS

Versions of Bible Used	Number of Hakka Presbyterian Congregations	Number of Hakka Congregations of Other Denominations	Total
Minnan	4	0	4
Minnan & Mandarin	6	0	6
Mandarin	18	33	51
Not indicated	2	8	10
Total	30	41	71

For hymnals, the Hakka churches have a wider choice. The Presbyterian Minnan hymnal is available in both Roman script and in Chinese characters. The latter is easier for paraphrasing into Hakka. Hakka churches of other denominations use their own denominational hymnbooks, all in Mandarin. It is quite a disheartening experience to sit in a Hakka church and listen to Hakka Christians trying to read Hakka out of non-Hakka Bibles and hymnbooks. They would stagger along through difficult places where each person gives a slightly different extemporized Hakka equivalent at a slightly different speed. It is really a miracle of God, wrought through the courage of Hakka Christians, that Hakka-speaking services exist at all.

MINNAN TAKING PRECEDENCE OVER HAKKA

Another outcome of the one-language policy is that, within the Presbyterian church, even in local congregations, Minnan seems always to take precedence over Hakka. Hakka-speaking congregations only exist in traditional Hakka towns or villages. In newly developed areas, such as the urban centers and the east coast of Taiwan, not a single Hakka congregation can be found. The sizable Hakka populations in these areas are supposed to be bilingual. Hakka Christians have to worship in Minnan or Mandarin.

Even the Hakka congregations are frequently under pressure to add Minnan or Mandarin in their services. In fact, it is not infrequent that the language of a Hakka meeting is inadvertently changed into Minnan because of a Minnan pastor or one or two new Minnan members. In some cases, like the Kao-shu church in Pingtung county which was started as a Hakka congregation, the Hakka language was given up altogether in church services.

Table 11, compiled from survey Questionnaire A, shows the situation.

Obviously this one-language policy has thwarted the development of any specialized personnel and efforts to win the Hakkas. It is largely responsible for the retarded growth of the Hakka church in Taiwan. The question now confronting us is, How did this one-language policy come into being?

IMPORTANCE OF THE HAKKA LANGUAGE UNDERESTIMATED

The reason most readily given for the one-language policy is that the Hakkas are bilingual, or are soon going to be. But is this a sound reason?

When missionaries first arrived in Taiwan a century ago, they found the Minnan speech, the majority language, was a convenient trade language learned by many. The fact that there were people movements to Christ among the ac-

TABLE 11

LANGUAGES USED BY HAKKA CONGREGATIONS
IN CHURCH MEETINGS

Language	Number of Hakka Presbyterian Congregations	Number of Hakka Congregations of Other Denominations	Total
All Hakka	8	10	18
All Minnan	5	1	6
Hakka & Mandarin	1	21	22
Hakka & Minnan	7	0	7
Minnan & Mandarin	2	1	3
Hakka, Minnan, & Mandarin	5	0	5
Not indicated	2	8	10
Total	30	41	71

culturized aborigines who had adopted the Minnan language probably added weight to the decision of carrying out the missionary effort in one language—Minnan. Anyhow, the idea of setting up a Hakka-speaking division of evangelistic work never occurred to those pioneers. MacKay wrote that "they [the Hakka] speak a dialect of the Cantonese. The younger generation learn the Hoklo [Minnan] dialect, and *in time the Hakkas may become extinct*"[4]

Through the years missionaries and ministers must have reasoned, as many still do today, that since many Hakkas could speak Minnan, evangelization could be done sufficiently well in one language, thus avoiding the tedious effort required to duplicate everything in another language.

This decision, however, was ill-founded. By anticipating a cultural change more than could be warranted, the early leaders of the church evidently underestimated the importance of the Hakka language. The result has been tragic. As late as 1953, when the Canadian Presbyterian missionary Hugh MacMillan wrote his book, *First Century in Formosa*, the Hakkas still appeared as a somewhat vague, little-contacted, remote people. Said MacMillan:

> Due to the remoteness of their upland villages from the main lines of communications and to their different vernacular from that used by the Fukienese [Minnan] Christians; also to the lack of missionaries with a knowledge of their language, little evangelistic effort has been carried out among them.[5]

It is true that some Hakkas have learned to speak good Minnan or even adopted the Minnan language in their daily lives; yet the fact remains that the Hakka population in rural areas still does not generally speak Minnan. Many Hakkas have only a simple knowledge of Minnan speech that is far from sufficient for delicate and complicated matters as personal salvation in Christ. Young Hakka Christians hesitate to participate in island-wide youth meetings because they do not speak Minnan and feel out of place. Old elders who do not speak good Minnan feel inadequate to go to the presbytery meetings. So even from a practical point of view, the one-language policy is untenable.

Why, then, has this policy been continued year after year and decade after decade?

A COURSE OF INTEGRATION

Interestingly, the church seems to have insisted on the one-language policy and followed a course of integration for the very reason of overcoming the difficulty in verbal communication. It has been hoped that by encouraging the Hakka believers to learn Christian literature in Minnan, the distinction between the two groups may be minimized so that the church may grow freely among both of them.

This, unfortunately, has led to a long-term objective, hidden in the Presbyterian church, of submerging the Hakka identity under the Minnan majority. One indication of this is that in the five-hundred-page *Centennial History of Taiwan*

Presbyterian Church, only two or three lines explicitly mention Hakkas at all. Another evidence is that when a certain foreign mission board proposed to the Presbyterian church some fourteen years ago that its missionaries be assigned the Hakka area as their specialized field of labor, the offer was turned down on the ground that this comity-like proposal was not in harmony with the established administrative procedures of the church. (The writer interviewed a pastor in November 1968 who was a member of the committee making that decision. Since this was a touchy matter, however, the resolution did not go into the official minutes.)

In 1958, when some Presbyterian Hakka laymen in Hsinchu area organized a "Hakka Evangelism Auxiliary Committee" out of their own zeal, they met a cold reception from the church authorities. The committee was in operation for only two years.

Another example can be added. Earlier in the chapter we indicated that some zealous Hakka ministers have adapted a number of hymns to the Hakka language. They have urged the church to publish these hymns. Counteracting this proposal, the 1968 general assembly resolved "to produce a new Mandarin hymnal for the convenience of the Hakkas, Highlanders, Mainlanders, and young people." In other words, no publication of a Hakka hymnal!

THE DETRIMENTAL EFFECTS OF INTEGRATION

Has the policy of integration accomplished the desired result? It seems not. In fact, the existing Hakka congregations have greatly suffered. Under the same general policy and same set of regulations, it is extremely difficult for a small Hakka church, without special outside help, to compete with its Minnan counterpart. Due to the difficulty of winning Hakkas into a Christian faith which is largely Minnan in coloration, Hakka congregations do not and cannot grow as fast as Minnan congregations. If a church cannot be self-supporting—and the small Hakka churches cannot be—then it cannot get its young Hakka-speaking preacher ordained, even if he is otherwise qualified. Talented Hakka workers have therefore to seek advancement by becoming pastors of large Minnan churches. The Hakka congregations, constantly lacking pastoral care, cannot grow in spiritual quality, either.

Blame is too easily put on Hakka ministers, often by careless non-Hakka observers, to the effect that the Hakka ministers are selfish in preferring to work in Minnan churches or going overseas as missionary pastors, instead of returning to their own needy people. Therefore *they* are responsible for the weakness of Hakka churches. This is too simplified a rationalization; it does not take into consideration the integration policy which, by keeping young Hakka preachers unordained, actually penalizes them if they choose to stay in Hakka congregations. Such critics have also overlooked the fact that for three years in seminary, Hakka preachers have received all their training in Minnan—a situation hardly conducive to their preaching in the Hakka tongue.

Comments are frequently made that the Hakka Christians are poor and stingy. Hakka churches do not grow because Hakka Christians do not give. Such a statement, for two reasons, should be seriously doubted. First of all, a church can be as poor or as wealthy as its members are. It need not and should not be otherwise. Poverty is not enough reason for lack of growth. Secondly, the Hakkas are certainly not stingy toward the expenses involved in their own religious ceremonies. Before Hakka Christians have a system of Christianity in their own language and are thoroughly taught in God's Word, they should not be blamed for a meager giving to the church.

In other parts of the world, illustrations can be found to show that an integration policy often retards church growth. In Guatemala, for example, the Indian believers have the Bible only in Spanish; becoming Christians means leaving their own culture. It is an open question whether they are truly resistant to the gospel. In Liberia, the inland tribespeople should not be judged resistant until more missionaries learn to preach in the local dialects. According to Wilhelm Fugmann, a German missionary in New Guinea who was for many years the administrator of the Lutheran mission there, the growth of the Lutheran church in New

Guinea at the present time is slower than it should be, and this can be ascribed to the lack of care given to the minority elements within the church of four hundred thousand members who belong to many tribes. Some tribes are 95 percent Christian, some are only five percent Christian; yet they have the same bishop, the same policies, and the same program. Though all are New Guineans, the fact that they are of separate tribes and that becoming Christian means adopting the language and culture of the already Christian tribe actually retards the growth of the church.

THE PROBLEM OF PEOPLE-CONSCIOUSNESS

Instead of solving the problem caused by the difference in languages, the attempt at integration has actually added more problems that have hindered the healthy growth of the Hakka church. This leads us to suspect that the real issue may lie deeper than the problem of verbal communication. Could it be that the basic harm done by the one-language policy is to ignore the strong people-consciousness which the Hakkas have—the consciousness of belonging to a distinct group, the sense of peoplehood, of which the language is but an expression? Could it be that the church has shown the worst kind of neglect over the Hakkas, the neglect of their ethnic self-image? Could it be that their resistance is but a result of such a neglect?

How strong is the people-consciousness of the Hakkas? To what extent should we allow it to affect our policies? The church has followed the course of integration on allegedly theological grounds. Should we not be united in Christ? Should we not consider the Hakka churches as the equal of Minnan churches? Under the present tide of ecumenism, can we afford to promote a separate Hakka church?

In the following three chapters, we will seek to understand the source and development of the Hakka people-consciousness, and to inquire into an approach under which the people-consciousness can be directed toward helping church growth. The ensuing conclusions will affect not only the Hakkas but also the many "resistant" peoples in the world whose consciousness of ethnic identity has been more or less neglected.

6

HISTORY OF THE HAKKAS

BEFORE MISSIONARIES ANYWHERE can really understand a supposedly resistant people, they must see them in historical perspective. As we now explore the stories of the Hakka people and try to delineate their "personality," our readers will be thinking of the ethnic group which they are called to evangelize.

HAKKAS AS SEEN BY FOREIGNERS

George Campbell, an English Presbyterian missionary, compared the Hakkas to the North American immigrants who refused to mix with the natives. He called them "a very distinct and virile strain of the Chinese race," and predicted that they "will play an increasingly important part in the progress and elevation of the Chinese people."[1] The Catholic Bishop Francis Ford noted that the Hakkas possess the "good characteristics of frontier people: a readiness to help one another, an ability to be satisfied with nature's harshest moods, a love of home that suffering in common begets, and a strict code of morals"—so much so that "the Maryknoller from Brooklyn often referred to the Hakka people as his 'kith and kin,' and admitted that he was prejudiced in their favor." Ford also said, "The Hakka Chinese should be of special interest to Americans because their history finds its echo in the lives of our own parents or grandparents . . . . They merit our special study."[2]

But not all the Western writers on the Hakkas made such favorable remarks. In some writings such as the following, the Hakkas are likened to gypsies, outcasts, Jews, untouchables, or rebels.

D. C. Boulger, talking about Hung Hsiu-chuan, the leader of Taiping movement, said that he

> had a very common origin, and sprang from an inferior race. Hung-Tsiuen, such was his own name, was the son of . . . a hakka, a despised race of tramps who bear some resemblance to our gypsies.[3]

James W. Davidson, while serving as consul of the United States in Taiwan, wrote:

> In China they (the Hakkas) were considered as outcasts . . . . They were driven about from place to place and, like the Jews, possessed no land they could call their own.[4]

Davidson's remark probably found its way into two other recent writings on Taiwan:

> In China the Hakkas had travelled from place to place like gypsies and had possessed no land of their own.[5]

> Of the population in 1945 [in Taiwan] . . . , with the exception of the 140,000 tribesmen in the mountains, forty percent were of Hakka stock, the untouchables of south China . . . . They were branded as "strangers" in their own country, hence the name Hakkas.[6]

In *Encyclopaedia Britannica* we find:

> HAKKAS ("guests" or "sojourners"), a people of south China . . . .
>
> According to tradition they were found in Shantung and other provinces north of the Yangtze river as early as the third century B.C. They fled south of the Yangtze to escape the Tartar, Mongol and other invasions of China. They would not submit to foreign rule, so were considered rebels and there was constant warfare with the prevailing powers.[7]

Whether these remarks are true or not, they certainly stimulate us to find out more about this interesting branch of the Chinese race and to discover historical factors for their "resistance." Similar low views of other resistant peoples may also have closed many doors for evangelization among them. For the missionaries, it certainly pays to gain a thorough and sympathetic understanding of the history and cultural background of similar less understood peoples around the world.

THE EARLY PERIODS (BEFORE A.D. 1644)

E. J. Eitel of the Basel Mission, one of the earliest Western writers on the Hakka people in Kuangtung province, observed that (1) they were "unmistakably thorough-bred Chinese," and (2) they were "altogether a separate branch, differing in character and manners from the other two races, the Puntis and Hoklos."[8]

The early history of the Hakkas has been well established from various evidences. In the fourth century A.D., people from all parts of north China moved southward in great numbers. Some of them came to the mountainous southwestern part of Fukien province, T'ingchou by name, during late ninth century. In those secluded mountains, they lived for over four hundred years, then moved again to the adjacent equally mountainous region in the northeastern corner of Kuangtung province, faithfully preserving their culture. This area, formerly Kaying prefecture of Kuangtung province, has for the last six centuries (since 1300) been the home of these conservative Hakkas—Sojourners—as we know them today. From there some of them migrated to other parts of Kuangtung as well as to neighboring provinces, including Taiwan, and even to faraway countries such as Malaysia, Thailand, and Indonesia.

CLAN RECORDS DISPLAY NORTH CHINA ORIGINS

The Chinese place considerable importance on keeping genealogical records; therefore it is not hard, at least to a certain degree, to trace the origin of any clan. In a paper read at a missionary conference in 1912 and later published in the *Chinese Recorder*, missionary George Campbell observed that "the Hakkas . . . take much interest in establishing their descent from purely Chinese ancestors." And he found that "the family traditions and the record of [some] families indicate that they came from Honan, the cradle of the Chinese civilization."[9]

Rudolf Lechler, one of the first missionaries to work

among the Hakkas, also found that "the most reliable sources for tracing the origin of the Hakkas in this province [Kuangtung], are the family records, which are religiously preserved by the heads of clans." After examining the records of some fourteen clans, he concluded that "it will be seen that the Hakkas descended from the north of China."[10]

Anyone seeking to understand the Chinese must search the dim reaches of antiquity. Clan records frequently contain references to the Chou dynasty (1100-221 B.C.). The Chinese clans have a tremendous sense of family history running back for three thousand years. Some of this may be legendary, but even so, it is of very great psychological importance in evangelizing the conservative Hakkas today. The gospel comes to men and women proud of their long and distinguished ancestry. The following two examples are from the fourteen records examined by Lechler:

Lai clan: Shantung province (Chou dynasty, 1100—221 B.C.); Fukien province; Kuangtung province (Sung Dynasty, A.D. 960—1280)

Lo Clan: Shantung province (Chou dynasty, 1100—221 B.C.); Fukien province (T'ang dynasty, A.D. 618—907); Kuangtung province (Ming dynasty, A.D. 1368—1644).

HALL NAMES REVEAL ORIGINS

Another source of data closely connected with the clan records is the "hall names" which clans inherit from the ancestors. These hall names are names of counties in Honan province or adjacent areas. A clan may have one or more such hall names, or one hall name may be used by more than one clan. Campbell cited the following examples:[11]

Liang clan: On-t'in Hall and Si-ho Hall
Yap [Yeh] clan: Nam-yong Hall
Lim [Lin] clan: Yin-chon Hall

These hall names add to the evidence that the Hakkas are descendants of renowned Chinese families in the north.

SOUTHWARD MIGRATIONS OF NORTHERN CHINESE

The center of the traditional Chinese culture is a region called Chung-yuan (Central Field or Central Plain) in north China. It lies just south of the Yellow River and is comprised of the whole province of Honan, with parts of Shantung, Hopei, Shansi, and Shensi provinces. The antiquity of this region can be seen from the fact that during the latter part of the nineteenth century, archaeologists found in Honan province some one hundred thousand fragments of oracle shells and bones dating back to Shang dynasty (1500—1100 B.C.).

The history of the Hakkas has to do with some large-scale southward migration of the population in Chung-yuan area. The first of such migrations occurred in A.D. 311 and after, when the nomad tribes in Mongolia succeeded in breaking into the Middle Kingdom and ruling temporarily over north China. The court of Tsin dynasty (A.D. 265—419) was forced to move southward, and with it went huge numbers of the northern inhabitants, especially the literati and well-to-do families, who decided to leave their old homes to seek a refuge in the more quiet and less populated south. No less than ten new counties had to be created to rehabilitate these refugees. This movement has similarities to the great migration of millions of Europeans to the new world during A.D. 1500—1900. Some clans of Honan people settled in Kiangsi province south of the Yangtze River, and later became the progenitors of the present-day Hakkas.

The second major event that had to do with the history of the Hakkas was the devastating rebellion during A.D. 875—884 led by Huang Ts'ao. His ravening troops looted and slaughtered through ten provinces and caused millions to leave home and seek refuge in more remote regions. This rebellion also hastened the downfall of the once powerful T'ang dynasty (A.D. 618—907), which was displaced by a series of five interim dynasties in the north (A.D. 907—960), plus six independent kingdoms in the south set up by former viceroys or governors.

These southern kingdoms, though not considered legitimate lines by Chinese historians, were actually "better governed and far more stable [than the north, and] it was in these states, which for the most part refrained from wars either among themselves or against the rulers of the north, that the culture and literature of the T'ang period was preserved in this dangerous period of confusion."[12] These kingdoms soon disappeared when the Sung dynasty (A.D. 960—1280) succeeded in reunifying the empire, but one of their remaining influences was the diversity of local dialects and customs which we still see persist in the south.

A REFUGE IN FUKIEN HIGHLAND (A.D. 900–1300)

Amid the widespread turmoil, one little paradise in the mountainous southwestern part of Fukien province fortunately escaped the Huang Ts'ao destruction. Therefore to this region, T'ingchou prefecture of Fukien province, flocked thousands of the inhabitants of the neighboring Kiangsi province who formerly came from Honan province in the north. Others from farther north also came to this area at the same time. In Hakka clan records, frequent references are made to the Huang Ts'ao rebellion as being the cause of their ancestors moving to T'ingchou.

In this secluded T'ingchou area, these refugees settled down for some four hundred years (A.D. 900—1300) throughout the Sung dynasty. It was here that a distinct subculture emerged which characterizes the Hakka people as we know them today.

FROM FUKIEN TO KUANGTUNG TO FOUND
A HAKKALAND (A. D. 1280–1644)

T'ingchou is connected by a small river toward the south with Kaying prefecture of Kuangtung province, so it was natural for the people in T'ingchou to develop in that direction when, for instance, the population pressure built up.

Kaying prefecture, called Moichu at that time, was an undeveloped area chiefly populated by aboriginal tribes— not ethnically Chinese. Small-scale migrations to that area took place almost immediately after the refugees began to settle in T'ingchou. In a Chinese source we read that

as early as 900 A.D. there were wandering farm laborers from

Fukien and Kiangsi. A census of Meihsien [Moichu] in 976 showed that there were 367 such "alien" and 1,210 "native" families.[13]

Another source says that

the country [Moichu] is extensive but the people are lazy, depending on wandering farmers from T'ingchou and Kanchou [in southern Kiangsi province] to till their soil.[14]

The same source indicates also that one hundred years after that, in A. D. 1078, there were 6,548 alien and 5,824 native families. The term *alien*, used in the sources quoted above to designate the sojourning population, is "Hak" or "Hakka" in Chinese. During the 1100s and 1200s, Moichu continued to be developed by the people migrating from T'ingchou.

Around A. D. 1280, Moichu became the battleground of the Sung faithfuls against the invading Mongols. About eight thousand "Hakkas" from Moichu followed the defeated Sung court all the way to the southern seacoast and died there. Moichu was destroyed by the angry Mongols who finally overthrew the Sung dynasty and set up the great dynasty of Yuan (A. D. 1280—1368). It was during the Yuan dynasty and the succeeding Chinese dynasty—the Ming (1368—1644)— that people came down from T'ingchou in large numbers to replenish the area's population. These Fukien mountaineers found no difficulty in developing the mountainous Kaying area, including Kaying prefecture and parts of the neighboring Ch'aochou and Huichou prefectures, to be their new home. Kaying has since become the Hakkaland until today.

ABUNDANT EVIDENCES IN CLAN RECORDS FOR

T'INGCHOU-KAYING MOVEMENT

The movement from T'ingchou to Kaying marked the real beginning of the Hakkas as a separate people. When George Campbell tried to trace the ancestry of the Hakkas, he found a major movement from T'ingchou to Kaying in the fourteenth century, some three hundred years before the first Pilgrims came to America. The majority of the Kaying inhabitants today can "count from seventeen to twenty-five generations in Moichu [Kaying], or an average of twenty generations, indicating a period of 600 years."[15]

Lechler made a more detailed report in the *Chinese Recorder* of his examination of clan record. The following is a summary made from his article: [16]

> Li clan: (to which belongs Lechler's catechist), descendants of the imperial family of T'ang dynasty: Shansi province, Chekiang province, T'ingchou prefecture, Shih-pi, Ch'ang-loh (Kaying prefecture, for five generations), Ts'ing-yuan (near Canton, for twenty-two generations)
>
> Hung clan (to which belongs Lechler's other coworker, as well as the famous Taiping leader Hung Hsiu-chuan): Shensi province, Szechuan province, Kiangsu province, Fukien province, Kaying, Hua-hsien
>
> Ch'en clan: T'ingchou (for 21 generations), Ch'ang-loh (Kaying prefecture), Sin-an
>
> Lai clan: Shantung province, Fukien province, Ch'ang-loh and Kui-shan
>
> Lo clan: Shantung province, Fukien province, Kaying
>
> Yen clan: Shantung province, Kiangsi province, Ch'aochou prefecture (Kuangtung province), Kui-shan
>
> Ho clan: Shantung province, Fukien province, Kaying
>
> Kiang clan: Yangtze River, Hai-feng (Kuangtung province)
>
> Hiu [Ch'iu] clan: Honan province, Fukien province, Kiangsi province, Kui-shan
>
> Ts'ao clan: Fukien province, Ch'ang-loh (Kaying), Poh-lo, Kui-shan
>
> Liang clan: Honan province, Kaying and Sin-an
>
> Chang clan: Fukien province, Kuangtung province
>
> Huang clan: Fukien province, Kuangtung province
>
> Tai clan: Fukien province, Kuangtung province

We see that out of these fourteen records examined by Lechler, at least seven clans—Li, Hung, Ch'en, Lai, Lo, Ho, and Ts'ao—moved from Funkien to Kaying (although their ancestors did not all come from Honan province and there is little mention of Kiangsi province either). Most probably the Liang, Chang, Huang, and Tai clans made the same move.

Prof. Lo Hsiang-lin, the contemporary Chinese authority on the Hakka people, has collected forty complete Hakka clan records in a book.[17] Ample evidence can be found in that book to confirm, beyond any doubt, that the main bulk of the present-day Hakkas moved from T'ingchou to Kaying. This important movement has very much to do with the formation of the Hakka peoplehood, as we will see in the next chapter.

SPREADING OUT FROM KAYING HAKKALAND

During the Ming dynasty (A.D. 1368—1644) the Hakkas dwelt peacefully in their new home in Kaying. But when the population grew too big to be supported by the limited amount of arable land, further movements became necessary. During the Manchu dynasty of Ch'ing (A.D. 1644—1911), the Hakkas moved out in large numbers.

TABLE 12

OVERSEA CHINESE AND HAKKAS

(1962 estimate)

Place of Residence	Oversea Chinese	Oversea Hakkas
Malaya	2,550,000	530,000
Singapore	1,200,000	350,000
North Borneo	89,000	15,000
Brunei	22,000	1,560
Sarawak	190,000	1,200
Indonesia	2,000,000	550,000
Thailand	2,500,000	500,000
Hong Kong	3,128,044	368,000
Macao	450,000	58,000
India	16,500	1,250
Vietnam	600,000	96,000
Burma	600,000	150,000
U.S.A.	52,501*	10,500
Britain	120,000	24,000
Canada	52,501	5,300
Africa	46,000	14,000
Totals	13,600,000	2,670,000

*Obviously a misprint.

At first the Hakkas developed toward the south and the southwest to the coastal regions of Kuangtung province. It was among the Hakkas who had moved to the vicinity of Hong Kong that the German missionaries began their work. These Hakkas formed hundreds of their own communities interspersed among the original Cantonese-speaking population in Kuangtung province. Some Hakkas went farther west to Kuangsi and Szechuan provinces and formed their settlements there.

Large numbers of Hakkas also moved overseas to Southeast Asian countries, and on to all corners in the world. Table 12, showing the estimated number of all Hakkas outside of China, is taken from Kuo.[18] While the figures are very crude and incomplete, they nevertheless give a glimpse of the general situation—the Hakkas form almost a fifth of the total Chinese in Malaya, Singapore, Indonesia, Burma, United States, and Britain.

NEW HOMES IN TAIWAN

Many Hakkas also came to Taiwan. Taiwan has been a Minnan island since Koxinga's landing in 1661. The Hakkas came between the early 1700s and the late 1800s to pioneer mainly in the undeveloped hill tracts left by the Minnans, and formed distinct hamlets and villages and towns of their own. Generally speaking, they inhabit the foothills between the Minnans and the Highlanders, although in the south large tracts of lowland paddy fields are owned by some Hakka farmers.

According to the general census taken by the government in 1956, the number of lowland Taiwanese of Kuangtung ancestry (taken as Hakkas) is 1,236,350, or 13.28 percent of the total population of Taiwan. (See App. B for details. A more recent general census was taken in 1966, but the results have not been published yet.) Assuming the same percentage, the Hakka population in Taiwan in 1967 was around 1,759,000.

In Taiwan, the Hakkas settled in three major areas. In the north, the Hakka areas can be well demarcated. They form about 44 percent of the population of Taoyuan county, 58 percent of Hsinchu county, and 67 percent of Miaoli county.

In the south, they live in Kaohsiung and Pingtung counties, densely concentrated in Mei-nung township (pop. 57,000, all Hakkas) and around Nei-p'u township, but generally in villages interspersed with those of their Minnan neighbors. In Hualien and Taitung counties on the east coast, the Hakkas are recent migrants from Hsinchu area, and are in closer contacts with the Minnans and the Highlanders.

HAKKA POPULATION IN THE WORLD

The population of the Hakkas in Kuangtung province has been variously estimated by early writers from 4,000,000 to 8,000,000. The 4,000,000 figure given by Stauffer[19] is probably most dependable. Counting other Hakkas dispersed in Fukien, Kiangsi, Hunan, Kuangsi, and Szechuan provinces, 5,000,000 should be a safe estimate for all Hakkas on China mainland in the 1920s.

During the past fifty years, the population has at least doubled, so that the current figure for the China mainland should be 10,000,000 or more. With the 1,750,000 in Taiwan and the 2,670,000 in foreign countries, a round-number estimate of all Hakkas in the world today should be 15,000,000.

Fig. 6.1. Hakkas in the World

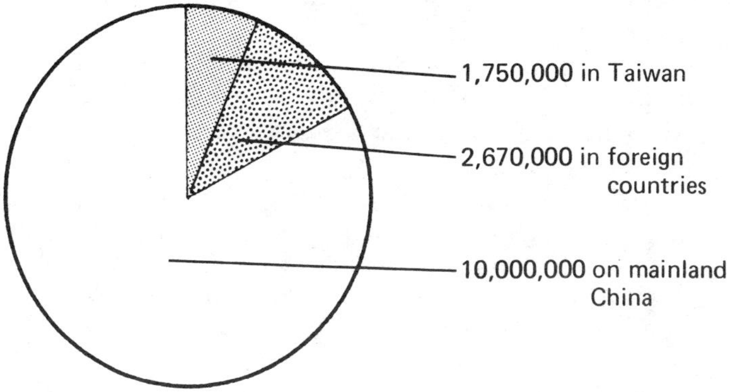

1,750,000 in Taiwan

2,670,000 in foreign countries

10,000,000 on mainland China

The Name "Hakka"

Perhaps frequent mention of migrations, abundantly found in Hakka clan records, is chiefly responsible for a widespread, inaccurate conception found in the writings of Westerners that a small tribe called "Hakka" existed two thousand years ago in north China, and has been roaming throughout the country until it finally reached Kuangtung province. The records of suffering, destruction, and slaughter can easily give the impression that this tribe has always been a despised and persecuted group. But this is far from the truth. The word *Hakka* was at first no more than a general term applied to any group of dislocated people, and it was not until the thirteenth century that it became curiously fixed to a particular group who alone continued to call themselves so.

The term *Hakka* appeared very early in Chinese historical records. An emperor of the Tsin dynasty (A.D. 265—419) decreed a system by which war refugees could be legally included in the local census register. (Normally, people could only be registered at the original hometowns. This somewhat resembles the situation under which Joseph and Mary had to go all the way to Bethlehem to register.) By this imperial decree, dislocated people were accorded the legal status of "k'eh" (sojourners); therefore their families were called "k'eh-hu" or "k'eh-chia"—the "households of sojourners." The practice of differentiating natives (chu) and sojourners (k'eh) in census registers was continued down to the thirteenth century.

The migration stories (or similar ones) which we just reviewed are actually a common heritage of almost all the Chinese who now live in south China. People other than the Hakkas can also trace their ancestry, from clan records, to Chung-yuan or elsewhere in north China. The periods of turmoil have caused migrations *from* many quarters *to* many quarters of the empire. As we have seen, the people dwelling in T'ingchou area during A.D. 900—1300 came from different places in north China. Driven by wars and calamities, they happened to live together in that secluded region—a situation not unlike the present-day Mainlanders in Taiwan.

There was not a special Hakka group, let alone a Hakka race or tribe, before the T'ingchou period.

MEANING OF THE WORD "K'EH" (HAK)

The Chinese word *k'eh* has a rather broad range of meanings. Basically it means "guest" or "outsider" as distinguished from "host" or "member of in-group." "K'eh-ch'i" (guest atmosphere) is the Chinese phrase for "politeness." The word *k'eh* is therefore used to designate recent arrivals or new-comers. To translate it "stranger" or "alien" sounds somewhat too strong and is subject to grave misunderstandings. In our present case, "sojourner" is probably the best translation.

"K'eh" is the Mandarin pronunciation. The same character is pronounced variously as hak, kaik, kih, kheh, khek, or kah in various dialects. "Hakka" is their own pronunciation of "k'eh-chia," households of sojourners.

POPULATIONS AKIN TO THE HAKKAS

Earlier in this chapter we noted that the present-day Hakkas are immigrants from T'ingchou to Kaying. The large-scale movements of population in Chinese history have produced many more millions of "sojourners" and it is to be expected that people settling near T'ingchou and Kaying areas, notably in Kiangsi and Kuangtung provinces, must have shared a similar background as the T'ingchou-Kaying group, and must be in many ways akin to the present-day Hakkas.

This was quickly observed by the early missionaries. They found that in Kiangsi province—north of the present-day Hakkaland—were millions of people speaking a variety of dialects very similar to that of the Hakkas.

Are these Kiangsi folks Hakkas? Yes, at first they were all "Hakkas"—sojourners. But when they blended with the natives, both Chinese and aborigines, they eventually dropped the tag and called themselves natives.

THE NAME "HAKKA" STUCK WITH ONE GROUP

It was with the group that had moved from T'ingchou to

Kaying that the designation "Hakka" had stuck. They did not seem to have called themselves Hakkas in their T'ingchou home. But when the T'ingchou immigrants first arrived at Moichu (Kaying), they automatically came under the Hakka category in census register. While their residence status changed gradually through the centuries, they somehow kept the designation of sojourners and continued to be called Hakkas both by themselves and by others.

But why did they not drop the seemingly derogatory label just as the others did? Eitel recorded the paradoxical fact that

> though this term (Hakka) was to all appearance given to this people by their enemies, the Puntis, at the time when the Hakkas first entered the Canton Province, and was certainly meant to be an humiliating term, the Hakkas themselves have adopted this name, even in the Department of Kiaying-chow, which the Hakkas generally consider to be their mother country.[20]

MacIver asserted that the name "Hakka, meaning as it does, 'stranger,' 'guest,' could not have been given as a name to the people by themselves." [21] Forrest was also puzzled by the question, "Why the Hakkas should be without a name by which to describe themselves other than one which meant foreigners," and raised a doubt as to whether the term *Hakka* when first applied really carried its literal meaning. [22]

From the discussion earlier in this chapter, we know there has not been a mix-up in orthography. Whatever the source of the term, the fact remains that the Hakkas have accepted it without the slightest dissatisfaction. So the only logical conclusion is: *They must have liked the name.*

But why did they like such a name? This leads us to the theme of the next chapter as we attempt to gain a deeper understanding of our peculiar friends.

7

A PECULIAR PEOPLE

EACH PEOPLE in the world is a peculiar people. Strong consciousness of peoplehood can scarcely be exaggerated even among the peoples who deny it. The Indians in Latin America may show a desire to become mestizos, but really they are only seeking the higher income and modern way of living, not the mestizo blood. The Japanese are well known for their ready acceptance of Western things, but this is actually a proof of their unusual ability to preserve their own traditional identity. The fact that many indigenous "new religions" spring up in the Japanese society testifies to the tenacity with which people cling to the things that are characteristically their own.

How the Hakkas Became Distinctive

To trace the formation of Hakka peoplehood is an interesting job. In reviewing Hakka history, one inevitably comes to some questions that demand further explanations. Why, for instance, are the Hakkas the only Chinese people who have retained the name of sojourners, whereas others who were once "sojourners" have all become "natives"? Why do the Hakkas alone treasure and cling to a Chung-yuan identity (there is a *Chung-yuan* monthly magazine in Taiwan published by Hakka people for the Hakka cause), whereas others who have just as much claim to Chung-yuan ancestry seem to pay no attention to it?

From the evidence that can be amassed, it seems very likely that the formation of this peculiar people was the result of two successive cultural conflicts: one with the tribal natives of Kaying, followed by a more serious one with the Cantonese.

LONG SECLUSION IN T'INGCHOU (A.D. 900—1300)

In the preceding chapter, we saw that the old Chinese cultures were better preserved in the south. We have also noted that the settlers of T'ingchou area were especially secluded from the rest of south China, as their mountain abode was far away from the capital of any of those southern kingdoms during the tenth century. This situation changed little in the three centuries that followed, so these secluded T'ingchou inhabitants had ample time to consolidate into a homogeneous unit, with an intense consciousness of being a separate people, and to develop their own culture quite independently of the more rapid changes in other parts of China. Of course they were not totally isolated, but the fact that they never adopted the widespread Chinese custom of female footbinding indicates a high degree of seclusion.

CONTACT WITH TRIBAL NATIVES IN MOICHU

During the Sung dynasty (A.D. 960—1280), T'ingchou people began to move to Moichu (Kaying) in small numbers. They came as wandering farmers, but among the immigrants there were also scholars. They were called sojourners— Hakkas—in the census register. The natives were chiefly tribal peoples such as Yao and She. These peoples were backward, but must have been quite numerous and strong. A minority having a higher civilization was confronted by a majority having a lower civilization. To the minority, the name "Hakka" was a matter of pride, a title of prestige, the designation of a nobler origin; and Hakkas they must remain! Such a situation seemed to have continued for three or four centuries, during which the Hakkas were always a minority; for around A.D. 1280, when Moichu was destroyed by the Mongols, we read that "the Yau [Yao] savages were emboldened to come down from the recesses of the mountains and attack the remnant of the people. They were only driven back after a pitched battle near the city."[1]

MISUNDERSTANDING CAUSES ANIMOSITY

The conflict of the Hakkas with the tribal natives alone,

however, would not have been sufficient reason for their retention of the name Hakka and their strong sense of identity with the ancestral land in Chung-yuan. Had it not been for an unfortunate happening in another cultural conflict, we believe they would have become "natives" of Moichu. But when these Moichu inhabitants slowly developed toward the southern coast, they met with other groups of Chinese—the Ch'aochou (Hoklo) group in the southeast, but above all the Cantonese, the majority group of Kuangtung province. We have reason to believe that, chiefly because the Hakkas did not practice footbinding, a prejudice against them was immediately formed in the mind of their new hosts—the Cantonese, or Puntis (local people, natives). In those days, from the viewpoint of an average Chinese, girls with unbound feet were either barbarians, tribal aborigines, or low-class laborers and servant girls. No girl with natural feet could be the bride of a decent Chinese wedding. So it was quite possible that from the very beginning of their contact with the Cantonese, an erroneous notion began to spread around: The Hakkas are tribal people from Fukien.

This mistaken idea even crept into some writings in English, as we find Oehler saying that "among authors writing without accurate knowledge of the Hakka history, the assertion is often found that the Hakkas belong to the aborigines of that province [Fukien], and are not really Chinese at all—an idea which the Punti, who are disinclined toward the Hakka, have always been ready to endorse."[2] One reason that had prompted Campbell to write his article was the "current misconceptions about the Hakkas" and the fact that "many who speak with authority on Chinese subjects have made absurd mistakes about this numerous, intelligent, and enterprising race."[3] Following this, Campbell mentioned that a government-sponsored textbook in Kuangtung contained a statement to the effect that the Hakkas and the Hoklos (Ch'aochou people in this occasion) were not of Chinese stock, but of a tribal origin in Fukien. Another writer tried to make the Hakkas and Hoklos of mongrel descent—half Chinese, half tribal. Erroneous ideas such as these, once started, have stayed stubbornly on. Just a few years ago, in Taiwan, a magazine writer put the Hakkas outside of the category of Han race (ethnic Chinese), causing no small protest from the Hakkas.[4]

To be called non-Chinese or mongrel is to a Chinese a grave insult. The reaction on the part of the Hakkas has been strong, too. A weaker group might have been totally demoralized under the situation, but not the Hakkas. On the one hand, it made them treasure all the more their pure descent from north China, and cling all the tighter to the name Hakka which had distinguished them from the tribal natives in Moichu. On the other hand, they were all the more conscious of their own mistreated minority status, and developed a resentment against the Puntis.

Such misunderstanding and resentment, together with the impossibility of intermarriage because of a difference in the size of the bride's feet (foot-binding in China was not done away with until the end of the nineteenth century), practically closed the door of mutual assimilation. Animosity between the Hakkas and Cantonese continued to grow worse and worse.

ECONOMIC CONFLICTS

Another reason for the animosity was economic. The surplus Hakka population was pushing forward all over Kuangtung and into Kuangsi to search for new settlements. Being industrious and frugal, the Hakkas had little difficulty outworking and eventually displacing the Puntis as landowners. The latter, of course, did not like such "intruders," and "fearful fights are recorded as the result of this pushing forward of the Hakka."[5]

BLOODY LOCAL WARS

The increasingly frequent fights between the two peoples finally broke in local wars. The largest one occurred in the Chao-ch'ing area southwest of Canton, where Hakkas and Puntis lived interspersed. It caused the loss of one hundred fifty thousand lives during 1854—1866, and doubtless added to the intense people-consciousness of the Hakkas. Lechler made a brief description of this terrible event:

The Taiping Rebellion [though led by Hakkas] . . . spread to the perfecture of Shau-hing [Chao-ch'ing] and found numerous adherents among the Punti people, whereas the Hakkas [there] remained loyal, and assisted the Mandarins against the rebels. This exasperated the Puntis very much, and they swore vengeance against the Hakkas. When the Taiping movement drew north, . . . the Puntis commenced hostilities with the Hakkas. The district of Hoh-san was the first in which disturbance broke out, and the fortunes of war were variously experienced on both sides, until finally the Puntis, being stronger in men and means, conquered the Hakkas in this and other districts, and expelled those who were not killed . . . . Tens of thousands were slain with the sword, untold numbers died of hunger, cold and general privation; again others perished by sickness. Many were taken captive and sold to the coolie ships at Macao . . . . Some made good their escape and went to Hainan, Saigon, and Singapore.[6]

The war was not over until finally, in 1866, the governor of Kuangtung succeeded in reaching an armistice. A portion of Hsin-ning county was marked out to form a new county of Ch'ih-ch'i to rehabilitate the Hakkas. The government also provided two hundred thousand taels of silver to pay travel expenses for the Hakkas who were willing to migrate elsewhere. This was the occasion in which great numbers of Hakkas moved to southwestern part of Kuangtung, to Hainan island, and overseas.[7] It was probably through this internecine war that many people got the wrong impression that the Hakkas have been the object of persecution since the third century B.C.

PEOPLE-CONSCIOUSNESS AND ITS EXPRESSIONS

Thus through being misunderstood and despised by others, through a sense of insecurity and the consequent need for protection, through the mutual help and suffering as a minority, and through the series of fights and wars, the Hakka people were welded together into a strong and solid bloc. All the environmental factors seemed to converge on developing a full consciousness of belonging to a unique people. "We are Hakkas" was stamped indelibly in the heart and mind of every one of them.

One could go too far in emphasizing the uniqueness of one particular people. In these days with the impact of industrialization on the one hand and the governmental emphasis on nationalization on the other, the division lines between peoples are becoming less noticeable, and in time, we hope, may disappear all together. The reason we have included here a review of the history of such animosity is not to endorse the old quarrels and hatred. We would love to bury and forget those unpleasant memories, were it not for the fact that knowledge of these historical backgrounds and lingering sense of animosity is necessary for a sympathetic understanding of the Hakkas. Their people-consciousness, which has persisted until this very day, has most important bearing on church growth among them.

The Hakkas express their people-consciousness in a variety of ways and in varying degrees. The following examples are sufficient to indicate the strong desire with which the Hakkas seek to preserve their own identity.

"GROUP-CONSCIOUS" RATHER THAN "REVOLUTIONARY"

The fact that the leaders of the Taiping movement were Hakkas gave rise to the common notion that the Hakka people are revolutionary in nature. For instance, in Little's *The Far East* is found the statement, "The Hakka section of the province[Kuangtung]was the cradle of the great Taiping Rebellion, and its people are always strongly inclined to revolutionary schemes."[8] It is true that the majority of Taiping soldiers were also Hakkas, but as we can see from Lechler's statement, quoted in the foregoing section, the Hakkas also fought on the government's side when and where the Puntis joined the Taipings. In other words, so far as the Hakkas were concerned, group-consciousness was still the main force at play. It can be said that the Hakkas have influenced the Taiping movement, but the opposite is scarcely the truth.

THE HAKKA MARTYRS IN TAIWAN

Let us move the scene to Taiwan now. Here again, the

Hakkas were in the minority, the chief power being the Minnans. During the 1700s, there were frequent clan fights between the two peoples, as well as numerous insurrections against the Manchu rule. When the insurrections were started by the Minnans, notably the two largest ones in 1721 and 1786 (led by Chu Yi-kui and Lin Shuang-wen respectively), the Hakkas chose the government's side and organized volunteers to fight the rebels. Such pro-government volunteers were granted the title "Yi-min" (righteous people) by the court, and were rewarded with both money and honor. In these instances, we can see again that what mattered most to the Hakkas seemed to be the solidarity of their own folk.

These martyrs have been widely worshiped by the Hakkas. In practically all Hakka communities throughout Taiwan, shrines and temples are built and dedicated to Hakka martyrs who died either in clan fights or as heroes against Minnan rebels. These martyrs are collectively called "Yi-min-yeh" (Their Excellency Righteous People), which has become one of the chief deities dear to devout Hakka hearts.

Of all these martyrs' temples, most important is the one located in Hsin-p'u township, Hsinchu county, just a few miles east of the main highway. The writer made a special trip in 1968 to visit this temple. It was not a worship day, so the place was quiet. The temple is located in the back of a clean and spacious front yard. Inside the temple there is no idol. In the main shrine in the center is placed a large tablet, elaborately carved and painted, with the following inscription:

"Ch'ih-feng Yueh-tung Pao-chung Yi-min Wei"

(Seat of "East-Kuangtung Righteous People with Special
Commendation for Loyalty,"
[A title] Conferred by His Imperial Majesty)

In the minor shrines, there are tablets for Fu-teh-cheng-sheng (a folk religion deity), Kuan-yin (Avalokitésvara), King of Three Mountains, Sheng-nung (god of fertility of soil), one Buddhist priest, and several donors.

Eighteen Hakka communities in Hsinchu county take

turns to carry on a large-scale worship ceremony every year on the twentieth day of the seventh lunar month. Religious offerings include some 800 hogs and 10,000 domestic fowls which are consumed in the feasting. Every year this worship ceremony attracts some 30,000 faithful pilgrims as well as numerous spectators from all parts of the island.

In the past, the Hakka militia in southern Taiwan was organized into six regiments called "Liu-tui." Today, while the military significance has long been lost, the "Liu-tui Association" still functions to promote the welfare of the Hakka residents.

MAINTENANCE OF HAKKA IDENTITY AND UNITY

The Hakka consciousness can also be seen today in local elections in Taiwan, especially in Taoyuan county where half of the townships are Hakka and the other half Minnan. Hakka votes invariably concentrate on Hakka candidates. In a recent issue of *Chung-kuo-shih-pao* (China Times) (1968), a daily newspaper published in Taipei, there was a record of injunctions given by top congressmen to the people of Taoyuan county for more harmony and cooperation between the two groups.

The writer was told by a Hakka pastor in southern Taiwan that in the grade schools in his town, Hakka children do not mix with Minnans. Hakka students often prefer to walk a longer distance to go to schools where the Hakkas are the majority.

A conspicuous Hakka vocational unit in Taiwan is the railroad workers. In ticket offices and on the trains, everywhere you see Hakkas. You may not notice it at first, but before long they begin talking among themselves in their own tongue.

THE HAKKA LANGUAGE

Language is another important sign of group identity. Recently the writer was sitting in a meeting of Hakka pastors. They talked Hakka, of course. But in the middle of a heated discussion, someone used Minnan language to quote what a

Minnan had said, and the language of the meeting drifted into Minnan, in which these pastors are just as fluent. The discussion went on for five minutes, when someone called out in Hakka, "Let's speak Hakka!" and they switched back to Hakka immediately.

Upon hearing the Hakkas talking, one who knows easily detects a similarity between Hakka and Mandarin, and rightly suspects the northern origin of the Hakka people. Forrest states that the Hakka language "stands between northern Chinese and Cantonese, and in the matter of innovations, closer to the former . . . . It is much more in the direct line of derivation from old Chinese."[9]

The ancient Chinese has eight tones. All of these are preserved in contemporary Cantonese; seven are in Minnan (Amoy); while in standard Mandarin, based on Peking dialect, there are only four. Hakka has six tones—four of the Mandarin ones (with different values, however) plus the two entering tones with abrupt endings in -p,-t,-k, which have been lost in modern Peking speech but still prevail most everywhere in south China.

While geographical variations do exist both on the mainland and in Taiwan, the Hakka language as a whole is quite uniform. Not being a language of commerce, Hakka is not spoken by many non-Hakkas.

PRESERVATION OF ANCIENT CHINESE CULTURAL TRAITS

We have seen that the ancient Chinese culture, preserved by the secluded progenitors of the Hakkas, had much to do in the development of Hakka people-consciousness. But the people-consciousness, in turn, also causes the Hakkas to be more conservative in the ancient cultural traits. Following are a few examples.

DISPOSITION OF A MOUNTAINEER

"The Hakkas are the cream of the Chinese people." This is a comment made by an early missionary, Mr. Spiker, quoted by Huntington [10] to support his theory of natural selection of races, which maintains that when an area suffers famines or other calamities, it is the strongest element of the population that migrates to other places to seek new resources for existence. Therefore the more desirable characteristics such as bravery, independence, courage, vigor, aggressiveness, are to be found in those who have moved far to escape natural disasters.

The Hakkas have largely preserved these characteristics by being mountaineers both on the mainland and in Taiwan. The Hakka settlements in Taiwan are located chiefly in hilly regions sandwiched between Minnan communities on the lowland and the territory of the Highlanders up in the mountains. Campbell said of the Hakkas:

> More fearless and self-reliant than town dwellers, they have all the love of liberty which characterizes mountaineers the world over.[11]

One side of the mountaineer's disposition is simplicity. He does not like crooked or round-about ways of dealing with people. He may lack tact, but he will not use tact to take advantage of others either. Because of this simplicity, he has no way to win the battle of life except to work very hard. He has developed a sturdiness that has enabled him to endure and overcome the hardship connected with his rugged life.

Out of the school of hardship has emerged the strong personality characteristic of the Hakka. He is not afraid, nor does he hesitate, to fight against people or nature in order to defend his right. At times he may be contentious; you will find him stubborn and arguing with you when he is not convinced that your way is the right way. He will not bend under pressure but may be moved by an act of kindness.

The hard life has also trained them to be very slow to spend money, and not a few ministers have attributed the weak financial condition of Hakka churches to this habit of frugality.

The Hakka habit of a daily hot bath, men and women alike, has been the object of much commendation by foreign missionaries. Plenty of water and a convenient bathtub are necessary parts of a Hakka house.

THE HARD-WORKING WOMEN

Another ancient characteristic preserved in the Hakka life is the hard-working women. All Hakka women work—wealthy and poor, gentry and peasantry, mothers-in-law and daughters-in-law. The writer was told by a minister about a lady whose husband is the principal of the local grade school. Despite his position and prestige in the commmunity, she works regularly in her banana fields—something quite unimaginable in other Chinese communities. Any visitor to a Hakka area cannot but be impressed by the healthy, strong, self-respecting women who play a much more important role in the family life than do other Chinese womenfolk.

EMPHASIS ON CLASSICAL EDUCATION

In general, the Hakkas have been diligent in getting Confucian education, since competence in the classics helps demonstrate their descent from the northern literati. Ancestral halls in Kaying were widely utilized as school buildings, and that prefecture has been well known for its atmosphere of learning. According to a Chinese source quoted by Shih,[12] out of the thirteen *chin-shih* (highest degree passed by court examination) in Kuangtung of the year 1752, six of them were Hakkas. Huntington wrote that

> another notable fact among the Hakkas is the prevalence of education. In their central district it is said that about eighty percent of the men can read and write, a greater percentage than in any other part of China. At the present time in their main town of Kia-Ying, which is only a little place with 10,000 or 20,000 people, there are, if I remember rightly, some 3,000 pupils in what are known as middle schools, that is, above the primary grades. At any rate they gather there from the little villages for many miles around to such an extent that almost nowhere else in China do so many pupils come from so small a population.[13]

EMPHASIS ON FAMILY AND CLAN LIFE

Another area of traditional Chinese culture which the

Hakkas excel in preserving is the emphasis on family and clan life. Children are taught to abide by the authority of parents and clan leaders. People of the same clan like to live together in large extended families. In Lu-feng county in Kuangtung, for example, the P'eng clan is called "P'eng Pan Hsien" (P'engs of half a county) because the clan numbers some 200,000 among the county's population of 400,000.

Keeping clan records is a matter of extreme importance. No Hakka should forget his proud descent. In Hakka villages in Taiwan, hall names are seen everywhere inscribed or written over gates. This practice of using hall names to indicate ancestral counties in north China is common among the Chinese in the south. The Minnans, for instance, use them on lanterns for funerals or festivals, as well as on tombstones. But the Hakkas in Taiwan are most faithful in putting hall names on the gates of their homes.

Then the most important of all: ancestor worship. A government official at a Hakka rally in Taiwan said: "We Hakkas boast three large-size things in every home—a large bath-towel, a large pair of women's feet, and a large ancestral tablet." Lechler observed that "the ancestor worship in the houses, in the ancestral halls, and on the hills where the tombs are, form such an important part of their religious duties, that these are always the last things from which they will separate, in case of conversion to Christianity."[14] Because this aspect of their life has so much to do with the prospect of church growth among them, we will give a full chapter to it (see chapter 9).

Connected with ancestor worship is the belief in geomancy (*feng-shui*) in which the Hakkas are well known for indulging themselves. A geomantically lucky site for the tombs of the deceased will—they believe—not only give the dead better rest, but also ensure continued prosperity of the entire posterity.

ONE-THOUSAND-YEAR-OLD FASHION IN CLOTHING

A bizarre costume dating back to the T'ang dynasty (A. D. 618—907) can still be seen on some old women in Mei-nung township, one of the largest concentrations of Hakka population in southern Taiwan. It is a long, loose, blue jacket with broad edgings and pretty buttons. A Hakka pastor presented to the writer one such dress which was a part of his sister's dowry. Just one generation ago, Hakka girls returning home from boarding school had to change clothes on the train before arriving home. As a whole, the Hakkas cling more tightly to traditional clothing than do the Minnans.

HAKKA SONGS AND FOLKLORE

No talk on Hakka culture is complete without a note on the famous Hakka songs. Eitel said, "The Hakkas are, as a whole, a singing people like the Germans."[15] He translated a long popular ballad[16] to show the importance of Hakka songs as "the surest index of the national character."[17] In *China Review* around the years 1882—1884, one can find a dozen pages of Hakka songs selected and translated by missionary writers. The Hakka people are quite unique among all Chinese in preserving until today the ancient custom of folk singing which we see in *Shih-ching* (Classic of Songs) edited by Confucius twenty-five hundred years ago.

Hakka songs are sung and enjoyed by all Hakkas—literati and commoners, men and women, old and young. The fact that this custom has survived for centuries indicates that the entire people considered it an integral part of their culture.

Hakka songs are most frequently heard in the mountains where the women are working hard. Therefore these songs are often called *san-ko* (mountain songs). Singing helps pass the time when working and alleviates physical fatigue. Singing is also a good means by which young men and women can exchange romantic messages. A large number of the songs are love songs.

Hakka songs are sung impromptu. Here is a way for an illiterate girl to demonstrate her brightness. A song is usually four lines in rhyme. This is one of the most popular forms of poetry developed in T'ang dynasty (A.D. 618—907). A few samples are included in Appendix C.

Like other Chinese, the Hakkas enjoy a rich heritage of folklore. An interesting story, telling about the origin of the Hakkas, is also included in Appendix C.

Many minority peoples in the world have songs and stories like these. They should not only be read as folklore, but as indicative of a distinctive people-consciousness which must not be allowed to prevent its owners from receiving the blessing of Jesus Christ.

PEOPLE-CONSCIOUSNESS NEGLECTED BY THE CHURCH

What bearing does the strong people-consciousness of the Hakkas have on church growth? Has it been a help or a hindrance?

If there had been only Hakka people living on the island of Taiwan when missionaries first arrived a century ago, the growth situation of the Hakka church would have been very different. The result would have been at least comparable to that of the Hakka church on the mainland. But unfortunately the church in Taiwan, first established among the Minnans, has paid little attention to respect for the Hakkas as a proud, separate people. The Hakka church has always been a part of Minnan church. Even the Hsinchu presbytery, located in predominantly Hakka areas, is largely controlled by non-Hakkas. The one-language and integration policies indicate that the church, under the dominance of Minnans, has totally overlooked the people-consciousness of this edgy minority.

The Hakkas have never been reached as a people. Their desire to preserve their own identity has been rejected and denied. Their sense of peoplehood has been continually infringed. Is this not a serious neglect on the part of the church? It is nothing short of a tragedy that the people who are so conscious of themselves have had that consciousness so steadily ignored in the vital matter of leading them to the Saviour of their souls.

In this light, the apparent "resistance" of the Hakkas—and the meager growth of their church—need little further explanation. Attitudes such as conservatism, stubbornness, and exclusiveness are but various expressions of the ignored peoplehood. Worse yet, these expressions have often been taken as proofs of their "resistance"—only causing more neglect.

A Common Dilemma

Such is the people, a peculiar one, a strongly self-conscious minority precariously maintaining its identity in the midst of a dominant majority. The dilemma, clearly seen in the Hakka-Minnan situation in Taiwan, is a common one found in most lands of the earth. How to break through the vicious circle and cause the church to grow vigorously should be a vital concern for all Christian workers who are facing similar situations.

8

HARNESSING
PEOPLE-CONSCIOUSNESS
FOR CHURCH GROWTH

PEOPLE-CONSCIOUSNESS can work against church growth; it can also work for church growth. The rapid advance of the Korean church, for example, has been enhanced by the people-consciousness of the Koreans under the tragic rule of the Japanese. Can the strong people-consciousness of the Hakkas be also directed toward helping them to accept the Gospel of Jesus Christ?

Two early missionaries on mainland China testified that the people-consciousness of the Hakkas had been a factor in their responsiveness. The Reverend R. Lechler of the Basel Mission said:

> On the whole the Hakkas are not as bigoted as the Puntis, and the gospel has found easier access to them than to the latter. It is also comparatively easier to make friends of them than of the Puntis. It is perhaps owing to their standing constantly in fear of their own countrymen, the Puntis, that any sincere sympathy which is shown them by foreigners finds more reciprocity, and is thankfully availed of.[1]

The Reverend F. Hubrig of the Berlin Mission found exactly the same situation. He stated that in south China Christianity had found an entrance especially among the Hakkas who were being mistreated by the Puntis and were more inclined to associate with the foreigners.[2]

We saw in Chapter 3 that the growth of the Hakka church on mainland China was the result of evangelistic and church-planting efforts directed to the Hakkas as a people. Both the Basel Mission and the Berlin Mission were started as Hakka missions. The English Presbyterian Mission opened its first Hakka station in 1870, and eleven years later, in 1881, set up a separate Hakka mission. These missionaries did all their work in Hakka, and published for the Hakkas two versions of the Bible (Hakka and Wukingfu) in addition to all kinds of Christian literature. The work was for the Hakkas—and Hakkas alone. Everything was designed with the Hakkas in mind.

Should not the Hakkas in Taiwan receive the same help? Can we not so revamp our methods that the Hakka people-consciousness, instead of obstructing church growth, may actually enhance it?

NEED FOR A SEPARATED APPROACH TO THE HAKKAS

In the foregoing chapters, we have seen that as long as the Hakka church is only a part of Minnan church, the Hakka people-consciousness is being neglected and stands in the way of the conversion of the Hakka people. Such a situation has produced the erroneous idea that to become Christians is to cease to be a good Hakka. This is certainly not what has been preached verbally, but this may well have been the most impressive message that the Hakkas have received from the church.

To pay due respect to the people-consciousness of the Hakkas, the first step is to employ what can be termed a "separated approach" in which we visualize a distinct part of the church, including personnel and various activities connected with evangelization, to be largely separated from the Minnan apparatus and exclusively directed toward the Hakkas. This means to recognize their sense of being a distinct people and their desire to preserve their own identity. This is to ensure that Christianization does not become a synonym for deracination or detribalization, and when individuals accept Christ, they will remain good sons and daughters of their own culture—be it Hopi, Hottentot, or Hakka. This also requires that a multitude of Hakka churches be planted in which Hakkas can be as thoroughly Hakka as Englishmen are English while worshiping in Anglican churches. When a Hakka inquirer comes to a Christian worship service, he must feel he is among his own people, and his people-consciousness is being enriched rather than improverished or even put aside. Such an approach, we believe, is the urgent need of the moment.

Examples can be found in the mission fields to indicate that when non-Christians can come to Christ without crossing social or cultural barriers, church growth is usually assisted. When a missionary in Ghana was careful to recognize the cultural difference between the town dwellers and the villagers, and geared his evangelistic effort to the latter in 1966, a steady growth of the country churches took place.[3] Muslims have been regarded as hard soil for the seed of the gospel but, during the past two or three years, thousands of them in Indonesia became Christians. They came in groups so that the difficult step of going against their own societies was avoided.

TELLING THE GOSPEL IN NON-CHRISTIAN HAKKA HOMES

During my field survey trips in Taiwan, I have found ample evidence to warrant the advocating of a separated approach to the Hakkas. Let me share one or two instances which indicate that such an approach has good potential for a greater result in church growth.

Quite contrary to my expectation, I constantly found a spirit of optimism expressed by those ministers of the gospel who were in daily contact with the Hakka people. The Reverend Ernest Boehr of The Evangelical Alliance Mission, one of the few missionaries on the island who have dedicated themselves to Hakka evangelization, said he had a standing invitation from a dozen non-Christian Hakka homes to hold meetings in which the gospel was the topic of discussion.

I visited one such meeting. Riding on Mr. Boehr's motor bike, we arrived at the Huang home in a small farming village on the suburb of Miaoli at 8:00 P.M. We were expected, and people were already gathered in the small living room. Five men and one woman, all over fifty years of age, formed the main group. Ten children sat in front on low stools, and some young women were standing at the door listening. Mr. Boehr was warmly received. After customary exchange of greetings, he started his discourse without singing a hymn or having a formal prayer. His topic for that night was "The Conscience." In fluent Hakka, he quoted the Bible to show that the human conscience, in which the Chinese put so much trust, was not an accurate standard at all. He used a Hakka saying to illustrate this point, and also mentioned the interesting coincidence that the Chinese character for "evil," *êh*, is composed of two parts which together mean "the heart of Adam." At first the group was not very quiet, but gradually they became interested. After finishing his twenty-minute talk, Mr. Boehr opened it up for free discussion in which the adults warmly participated to make it truly a dialogue on the gospel.

ENTRANCE OF THE GOSPEL INTO A HAKKA VILLAGE

Another experience that brought delight to my heart during my survey trips was to meet the Reverend Johan Johansen, Jr., a Norwegian Free Lutheran missionary, who speaks no Hakka and is doing Mandarin work in the commercial Hakka town of Tung-shih in central Taiwan. He had an unplanned beginning in holding gospel meetings in a certain Hakka village nearby. I had the privilege of being invited by Mr. Johansen to speak at one of his regular Sunday evening meetings in the home of Mr. Yeh, the headman of that Hakka farming community. Mr. Boehr, who later heard about it and went over to help, wrote the following account in his missionary newsletter in January, 1969:

> . . . Mr. Johansen . . . had a burden for the Hakka and similar ideas for reaching them. Finally on January 3, 1969 I went to Tungshih to see him and heard this fascinating and encouraging story:
>
> About two years ago a fortune teller was saved by the faithful testimony of his wife and burned all his books of the trade in public. Mr. Chan was baptized and took up dentistry. About the same time a Hakka lady living in the south became burdened for her relatives near Tungshih. As often as possible she would come north to exhort them to believe. She told them what she believed and said she would pray that they be

convinced. She also prayed the Lord to take away a brother's taste for liquor—and He did. Finally Mr. Yeh consented to her bringing a preacher to them.

As she set out last May she prayed for guidance. She had lived in the south so long she knew no preacher in Tungshih. The first church she came to was where Reverend Johansen ministered. She spoke no Mandarin and he no Hakka. Through an interpreter she told her story. Mr. Johansen said there was a missionary nearby who spoke Hakka. She said the Lord led her to him—was he not ready to do the Lord's will? Reverend Johansen was convinced it was the Lord's leading and began going to the Yeh home each Sunday evening.

The meeting is in the home of the brother who had his taste for liquor prayed away. He is also the district head. (140 families in the district.) A Christian Hakka lady who teaches in Reverend Johansen's kindergarten interprets his messages. Mr. Chan often goes along to help. When told of the tricks he used as fortune teller, the people were more convinced of the falseness of their old ways. They asked many questions about God and Salvation and other district families are listening too. Mr. Yeh refused to join in a year-end devil worship and exhorted his clan and other families to refrain too.

Mr. Johansen asked me to work with him in teaching and counseling these people. I am thrilled to work with him for it may be that the Lord has chosen to begin His great work among the Hakka in this little community 30 miles south of here [Miaoli]. I spoke to a packed house of eager listeners on January 12 and will be there again on January 19. We're counting on your prayers.

The meeting seemed to have gone on very well, for in February 1969 Mr. Boehr wrote again in his newsletter:

The evening of January 19 we were at Mr. Yeh's outside Tungshih. His home was crowded with 19 adults, 10 teens and 10 children. The oldest brother (74 years) attended for the first time. It was a warm time of fellowship.

It is to be noted that the approach just recorded illustrates *very* partially the full-orbed Hakka approach herein advocated. Not too much can be assured yet from these slight evidences of friendship—with not a single family baptized. Still, if this semiforeign approach wins marked friendship, how much more might a fully Hakka approach? If when the church appears foreign Hakkas respond, what will they do when it appears thoroughly Hakka?

THE BIBLICAL REASON

The necessity of a separated approach springs from the realization that conversion to Christ is a religious change, and a religious change alone. No one may add other unnecessary changes. In the Bible we see the Jews who had become Christians continued to be Jews as far as their culture, national consciousness, customs, political views, and most of their religious practices were concerned. No pressure was put on them to abandon their Jewish way of life. But when some Jewish Christians thought their culture (circumcision, pork taboos, and prohibition of interdining with the Gentiles) was a part of the Christian gospel and therefore should be forced on Gentile Christians, the apostle Paul fought the idea, disputing openly with Peter at Antioch (Galatians 2:11-16). McGavran has aptly argued the case as follows:

> The offence of the cross is one basic barrier to becoming Christian. To accept the truth that one is a sinner whose salvation depends not at all on what he does but entirely on his accepting what Jesus Christ has done for him on the cross, affronts his ego. To repent of one's sins and turn from them is another basic barrier to discipleship. Openly to confess Christ before men, be baptized in His name, and join the Church is a third obstacle. To those who accept the authority of the Scriptures, these barriers must remain . . . . But the Church and her emissaries are constantly tempted to add others. In most cases of arrested growth of the Church, men are deterred not so much by the offence of the cross as by non-biblical offences. Nothing in the Bible, for instance, requires that in becoming a Christian a believer must cross linguistic, racial, and class barriers. To require that he do so is to take the spotlight off the three essential biblical acts and place it on the requirement of men.[4]

A separated approach to a distinct people is right in God's sight. Theologically speaking, we must *not* require that Hakkas become Christians in an alien culture, be it English,

American, Japanese, or Minnan. It must be possible for Hakkas to become Christians within the distinctively Hakka environment. Indeed we have no right to do otherwise when cultural differences between two peoples still exist.

PRACTICAL ADVANTAGES

The need for a separated approach is not only theological, it is also practical. Conversion will be much easier when it is understood to be a religious change—a change in religious leadership, a change from gods and spirits to Jesus Christ the Saviour—without the addition of other cultural changes, or the requirement of crossing other cultural barriers.

The experiences of social workers can verify this point. Let it be clearly understood in the outset that church growth is a work of God to fulfill His own purpose. He does it in various miraculous ways far beyond our comprehension. The complete dependence on divine working, however, does not minimize the responsibility of God's faithful servants to utilize possible ways and means to accomplish the purpose—with the same kind of diligence with which a Christian doctor studies medical science.

Social workers have found that, in the matter of introducing technical changes in developing countries, unnecessary cultural accompaniments are hindrances. They recommend that

> where specific technical practices are to be introduced into a culture or a part of a society which has not hitherto used them, it is desirable to strip these technical practices of as many extraneous cultural accretions (from the lands of origin) as possible . . . . Extraneous and culturally destructive effects can be avoided by stripping each scientific technique to the bone, to the absolute essentials which will make it possible for other people to learn to use it, and to handle it in a living, participating, creative way.[5]

It is obvious that the acceptance of a new machine, for instance, is vastly different from the acceptance of salvation in Christ; but if social workers are careful to avoid cultural hindrances to the secular process of technical change, how much more should we be careful to avoid such hindrances to a process involving a much more important and difficult transformation? It is certainly our duty to see that only the "absolute essentials" of the gospel are transmitted to the people. No acculturation should be allowed to infringe upon the people-consciousness and thereby keep men and women from becoming Christians.

NEED FOR A HAKKA CHRISTIAN CULTURE

Under the separated approach, we have been advocating the preservation of the indigenous culture. But can the culture of a people remain intact when conversion to Christ takes place? Can new creatures in Christ coexist side by side with people clinging to the old way of life? Of course not.

Change in religion is a major change in an area of culture, and necessarily results in changes in other areas. Therefore the culture of Hakka Christians will be definitely different from that of Hakka non-Christians. But the differences should be in the realm of essential Christian faith and not in that of language, dress, marriage customs, and the like. The need is for a newly created Hakka Christianity in which a Hakka can be a good Christian *and a good Hakka* at the same time.

The gospel, with the historical facts of Jesus Christ, can never be changed. In no case should we compromise scriptural teachings with human customs. But at the same time, let us be diligent in seeking to maintain as much cultural continuity as possible. As a matter of fact, the Hakka church can well be the center where a new spirit of the Hakkas as godly Sojourners may be fully developed.

In constructing a Hakka Christian culture, language is no doubt an important ingredient. The gospel must be communicated in good Hakka vernacular to which the people are most accustomed. Efforts must be made to design a system under which all aspects of Christian activities can be carried out entirely in the Hakka language.

Challenging questions can also be asked in other areas like hymnody, for example, as to how Christianity can find expression in a way most congenial to Hakka culture. How can the great, transcendent love be sung to those and by those who are used to singing love songs in the mountains?

Christian forms of marriage, funerals, festivals, and memorials for the ancestors must be worked out. Much thought and effort should be given to development in these directions.

We should be careful, however, not to become too much involved or enthusiastic in such items of "indigenization." Nida pointed out that "attempts at functional substitutes by missionaries have been almost wholly unsuccessful."[6] The important thing to remember here, as will be discussed later in this chapter, is that the incorporation of elements from Hakka culture into the Christian life should be planned and developed by local Hakka Christians themselves, slowly if need be, under the guidance of the Holy Spirit.

PROBLEM OF CHURCH UNITY

In chapter 5 we touched on the policy of integration adopted by the Presbyterian church in Taiwan and the resulting difficulties experienced by the weak Hakka congregations. Suppose now the church were to change its policy and begin to win Hakkas into churches clearly separated from those of the Minnans, would that not encourage Hakka separatism and jeopardize the unity of the church? Are we not commanded to keep the unity of the Spirit? In Christ, we are taught, there is neither Jew nor Greek!

This is truly a legitimate concern. We realize that the policy of integration has been motivated by a genuine desire to attain universal brotherhood within the body of Christ. This desire is fully reflected in an official paper, entitled "Into a New Era Together," released by the Taiwan Presbyterian Church on the occasion of its centenary in 1965. In Chapter 1 of this paper, after briefly reviewing the demographic situation in Taiwan and pointing out possible tensions among the several ethno-cultural groups, the Presbyterian church urges the Christian community on the island to recognize such tensions and "respond creatively to them in the power of Christ . . . . For to be a community of Jesus Christ is to be a reconciled and reconciling community in and for the world."

The position represented in "Into a New Era Together" is

this: Growth of the church is important, but it should only grow *together* without making any distinction with regard to social or cultural divisions.

> Historically there may have been existentially justifiable reasons for the churches such as the Presbyterian, the True Jesus and the Holiness to concentrate their work among the Taiwanese, and for the more recently arrived churches and Missions to work among the Mainlanders. But to continue so to operate will be both impossible and intolerable because of the life and the mission of the Church . . . .

> Numerical growth is indeed an urgent and unfinished task for the Church on this Island. But in what way we are to grow in the midst of such a diversified population with its consequent manifold tensions is also an urgent and unfinished task. Is it to be "you in your corner and I in mine"? Or are we to grow together as a reconciled and reconciling community with the whole, though diversified, population as our field? To put it bluntly, are the Churches and Missions going to perpetuate group tensions by concentrating on this group or that group or are they going to be truly a reconciled and reconciling power among the diverse groups? . . . . "Here they cannot be Greek or Jew, circumcised and uncircumcised, barbarian, Scythian, slave, free man, but Christ is all and in all." (Col.3)

We fully appreciate this emphasis on our common call to the ministry of reconciliation. It is true that our ultimate goal is a complete brotherhood by which all individuals and peoples become part of Christ's body—the church. We also realize that even the secular world is hastening toward a larger and larger degree of unification of peoples. We have no doubt that great degrees of unification will take place in the future, both inside and outside of the church. It is the prerogative of the church not only to welcome such a unification, but to strive toward it.

STRIVING FOR TRUE UNITY

We must point out, however, that the church in seeking unity must be very careful to avoid the premature, ill-advised unification program which both retards church growth and actually adds to the spirit of division.

An Indian church in the Yakima Valley of the state of Washington provides a good illustration. During the late nineteenth century, many Yakima Indians became Christians and members of a Methodist church. Later when a number of white settlers joined the church and made it an integrated congregation, they gradually took over the leadership. The Indians felt intimidated, left the church, and joined a nativistic movement called the Shakers. "Integration, before both groups of Christians are ready for it, is often the kiss of death to the weaker party."[7]

Another example can be found in the black population in the United States. Admitting Negroes to white churches and organizations has been attempted, but while apparently a Christian solution, it has some weaknesses. It brings a minority of blacks into a church or other organizations where the dominant pattern and ethos is white. Obviously this brings no satisfaction to the Negroes who, on the contrary, are currently urging a great degree of separation— enough to enable *their* culture to survive and for them to feel at home.

In an article entitled "A Separate Path to Equality" appearing in a recent issue of *Life* magazine, a new approach to the old problem was voiced in the words of nine black spokesmen. Neither assimilation nor paternalism (characterized by a tiny black bourgeoisie and intelligentsia), nor an exodus to Africa or to a black partition in America, can offer a solution. The basic need, in the words of a black chemist, is to "rehabilitate blacks as a people . . . . We must deal with our problems as a whole—not individually as economic, political, or social. Integration is a total failure. We must continue as a separate entity."[8]

These words, however, should not be taken to mean that separation is to be permanent. They merely spell out the truth that an integration without sacrificing the interests of the weaker elements is only possible when such elements are well established in their own cultures among those of the stronger ones, so that mutual respect between peoples can be guaranteed. It is the bruised, about-to-be-submerged black culture that is at the root of the problem. Division is more likely to occur when integration is applied with coercion;

unity is better attained when each entity enjoys a healthy ethos of its own.

Will this separation in the church, though temporary, perpetuate the undesirable group tensions? We believe not. In fact, this temporary separation appears to be the very way in which the unity of the church can be truly attained, because it ensures full development of the selfhood of each group so that a unity that is fair to all groups is possible. Moreover this temporary separation, in as much as it helps Christianization of each people, can contribute tremendously to the reconciliation and integration of the various groups, because becoming Christian is the first step toward true brotherhood. Without Christ, no social action can solve racial problems.

In Taiwan, as long as the main blocs of population—Minnan, Hakka, Mainlander, Highlander—continue to exist, it is both legitimate and necessary to disciple these groups separately. The task of evangelization and church planting must go forward in each. No people should be neglected. To approach the Hakkas as a people and to produce thoroughly Hakka churches into which Hakkas may come with joy, will not only bring more of God's blessings to the Hakkas, but also bless the whole church in the long run.

NEED FOR AN ADEQUATE PATTERN OF CONVERSION

Another important way in which we may recognize and recheck the people-consciousness of those who belong to a distinctive group is to recognize their basic desire to maintain their group solidarity. Members of such a group often appear conservative, but really they are not quite so opposed to new ideas, if they know the changes will not threaten the continuation of their group life.

Solidarity of a group depends very much on a regular functioning of leadership. Something new will have a much greater chance of acceptance by the members of the group if the innovation is channeled through the existing leaders or at least with their approval. An impatient advocate of a new thing will likely want to get some young members of the group to accept the change quickly, but this will most certainly antagonize the leaders. They will then try to obstruct the innovation, not so much because they are against the new thing itself, but because they feel the process under which the innovation is accepted is a threat to their normal group life.

Here again, the experiences of social workers will confirm the conclusion that the process of an innovation is more important than its content.

INNOVATION THROUGH EXISTING SOCIAL CHANNELS

Social workers have learned that in order to ensure a successful technical change, the new thing must be introduced through the existing structure of the society. The following steps are recommended as essential:

1. The innovation should be channeled through the leaders of the society. "Experience in fundamental education in a number of countries points to the importance of working through local leadership, both for the acceptance of the project and for ensuring its continuing success." In the matter of introducing modern hygienic methods and other things to the people in Greece, the workers

> . . . realized that they had to use not impersonal scientists but people who were predominantly leaders, with scientific knowledge, people who were willing to go and live in the villages, and make the acquaintance of the peasants over coffee in coffee-houses. And the villagers fell in with the proposals for new hygienic methods and child care and artificial insemination because they had respect for and faith in the man who made the proposals. And where schemes introduced in the name of self-interest did not succeed, those introduced in the name of the respected leader did. "For your sake" is a common sanction.[9]

Another example is the introduction of vaccination to the Tiv Africans in Nigeria:

> In one region, the people refused to be vaccinated on the ground that the head of the family group had performed the appropriate akombo rites. The British administrator wisely dealt with this man as well as his senior, the head of the kindred. When the family head was persuaded that European

vaccination was advisable, he told his people, and they came easily of their own accord, without the need of persuasion.[10]

2. To help the leaders in their decision, a preliminary education and proper explanations are necessary. Here is an interesting example of getting around the difficulty through wise plans:

> In order to enlist the cooperation necessary to carry out the new measures, understanding of the existing patterns, as well as careful education, is needed. In Egypt and Arab Palestine, the proposed cooperatives are presented as the continuation of the traditional village cooperation. In support the Koran is cited, and the danger of the loss of land without cooperation stressed, with references to specific cases of such loss. The religious objection that cooperative credit societies charge interest on loans, going against Koran law, is counteracted by the argument that the interest charged is for the purpose of mutual aid, which is enjoined by the Koran.[11]

3. It is very important to invite the people concerned to plan together the proposed change.

> As a general recommendation . . . it is possible to say that it is dangerous ever to make any plan, or to try to execute any plan, without the active participation of members of the culture, of the particular professions, and of the administrative apparatus concerned; as soon as any planned change has a specific population group as its object, members of that group—through demonstration villages, pilot projects, etc.—must be brought into the planning . . . . The arrogant self-assurance which makes more industrialized countries force their methods on the less industrialized, the touchy eagerness to prove themselves that characterizes young nations, the missionary zeal of the apostles of the religiously orthodox, may all be welded into a working whole if exponents of each position plan together.[12]

Thus these social workers have found that a change is best made when the existing organization of a whole society (or at least a part of it) is taken into consideration.

THE ONE-BY-ONE PATTERN OF CONVERSION

So far the most common pattern of conversion to Christ among all the lowland Chinese in Taiwan (Mainlanders, Minnans, and Hakkas) is the one-by-one type prevalent in Western societies under which the gospel of Christ, with the challenge to receive or reject it, is acted upon by one individual at a time. Among the forty-three Hakka Christians interviewed by the writer, twenty-five are first-generation Christians. Each of them has come to Christ under this one-by-one pattern.

Such a pattern of conversion has met with great difficulties in non-western societies in which men and women are still under heavy influence of group life. Without going through the existing social channels, this type of one-by-one conversion comes into direct conflict with the people-consciousness of distinctive groups, Hakkas among them. The authority of the group is being challenged by the individual decisions and actions. Thus another wrong image of Christianity has been created: To be Christian is to desert your people. It is obvious that people-consciousness works against church growth under such a situation. The writer has met Christian workers testifying that many Hakkas like Christian preaching, but say they cannot "join the religion" (join the church).

The hesitant crawl of the Hakka church in Taiwan has definitely proved this. We have seen what a price the early Hakka Christians paid in order to be faithful to God. Though in the modern society persecution and ostracism may not be as severe as they were two or three generations ago, the one-by-one convert is in just as unfavorable a position as ever. After interviewing twenty-five first-generation Hakka converts, the writer has found the general pattern to be: (1) individual conversion meets with strong opposition and persecution from the family; (2) opposition subsides gradually in a period anywhere between a few weeks and a few years, resulting in a cold-war coexistence of the Christian with his non-Christian relatives; (3) the individual Christian in some cases succeeds in leading a few family members to Christ, but in most cases he remains a lone Christian living on the tolerated fringe of his society.

If we are not complacent with the present situation, we must seriously ask: Is one-by-one conversion the only legitimate procedure of leading men and women to Christ? Is the above-mentioned image necessary? Are ostracism and persecution absolutely inevitable? Should we not apply the principles of social changes to religious changes and seek a smoother pattern of conversion to Christ?

PEOPLE MOVEMENT TO CHRIST

Devoted Christian scholars have found that across the wide mission fields throughout the world, the normal process of Christian conversion has proceeded along a very similar course as a social or cultural change. When a distinctive people is approached as a people and not as individuals, or when their people-consciousness is simply allowed to persist, a very different pattern of conversion, termed "people movement to Christ" by Donald McGavran, has often been the result. Interrelated men and women from one people take up the challenge of the gospel together, think it through together, and decide together that they will become Christians, in much the same way they decide to accept a new machine or medicine. Here the people-consciousness is made to work in favor of the acceptance, and "loyalty to our people becomes the chariot in which Christ rides to the hearts of men."[13]

McGavran rightly insists that people movement, through which at least two-thirds of the Christians in Asia, Africa, and Oceania were converted, is a normal, indeed a major, pattern of Christian conversion — "the God-given way by which social resistance to the gospel can be surmounted."[14] This vitally important but different pattern of Christian conversion, often misunderstood and put under suspicion, is defined as follows:

> A people movement results from the joint decision of a number of individuals — whether five or five hundred — all from the same people, which enables them to become Christians without social dislocation, while remaining in full contact with their nonchristian relatives, thus enabling other

groups of that people, across the years, after suitable in-
struction, to come to similar decisions, and form Christian
churches made up exclusively of members of that people.[15]

Quite contrary to a common misunderstanding, a people movement is *not* a "mass conversion" by which a large number of individuals hastily professed Christianity under a kind of emotional pressure. A people movement, as McGavran explains it, is really "a series of multi-individual, mutually-interdependent conversions." Though a people movement eventually results in large number of conversions, quantity is not its primary characteristic. In fact a people movement normally starts with a small number of converts. Since the quality of Christians depends largely on adequate post-baptismal care and teaching of the truth, whether the Christians come by a one-by-one pattern or by a people movement pattern, there is no place for a charge against people movement on the ground that quantity is emphasized at the expense of quality. The main thing is for us to accept the fact that, in addition to the familiar pattern of one-by-one conversion, the people movement pattern is also a biblical, desirable, and effective means by which God brings men and women into His kingdom.

AIMING AT A HAKKA PEOPLE MOVEMENT

To a strongly self-conscious people like the Hakkas, the people movement approach would certainly be much more appealing than the one-by-one pattern. The gospel should be presented to large and small social units (extended families, kin groups, neighborhoods) rather than to lone individuals. Opportunities should be sought where the meaning of the gospel can be clearly explained to the leaders of such social units so as to remove any possible misunderstanding in their mind. The presentation should be made in the vernacular and in such a native way that the leaders feel they are capable of handling the new ideas and making proper decisions on them.

The first group of converts should be encouraged to stay in their original homes doing their accustomed work, to suffer persecution together if need be, and to bear testimony to the fact that becoming a Christian does not imply ceasing to be a Hakka. In fact, they have become better Hakkas because they are freed from sinful life. This will undoubtedly open a door in the hearts of many more from among their own folks.

An effective work of Christian teaching is essential for the continued growth of a people movement church. Instead of giving an impression that becoming Christian is merely to stop worshiping idols and ancestors, the positive values of Christian life, such as the privileges and blessings and liberations to be enjoyed, should be always in the foreground of the thinking of Christians as well as non-Christians. The adults should be the main object of Christian education for whom a set of teaching procedures should be specially designed. Natural leaders of the Hakkas — usually older men — should be recognized, trained, and placed in responsible church positions. Such a people movement will be more likely to produce an indigenous church, both in the sense of being self-supporting, self-governing, and self-propagating, and in creating out of the old way of life a new Christian Hakka culture which is well pleasing to God.

HAKKAS SEEN AS A NEW MISSION FIELD

In the light of the foregoing discussions, the conclusion is: The 1,700,000 Hakkas in Taiwan should be considered a new mission field which must be entered with bold, long-term plans under which church-planting evangelism, development of literature, and training of leadership, can be carried out systematically and patiently.

A special mission or agency is needed to coordinate the various efforts. A meeting was called in 1968 by the *Christian Tribune* in Taiwan to discuss Hakka evangelism. One of the conclusions was the urgent need of establishing a new Hakka evangelism board.[16] One pastor in the meeting pointed out that some time ago certain Hong Kong ministers wanted to help evangelize the Hakkas in Taiwan, but could find no entrance. If there had been a well-functioning agency, a helping hand such as this would not have remained unutilized.

A people movement is more likely to take place when

Christian workers "concentrate their attention on some one people . . . . Enough individuals and groups . . . must be converted in a short enough time and a small enough area so that each Christian comes into the church with some of his kindred."[17] This means perhaps a pilot project in certain Hakka communities where a concentrated effort can be made. Whatever the mode of work, the goal must be clear — a multitude of congregations made up of Hakkas, led by Hakka ministers and laymen having much pride of Hakka-hood, and rigorously engaged in bringing other Hakkas into the blessed fellowship of God's kingdom.

CULTURAL VACUUM

Amidst the rapid waves of industrialization, the old society in Taiwan is gradually disintegrating. Old customs and religious beliefs are on the wane; modern Western ways of life are making inroads. But this does not mean that the Hakkas will soon cease to be a distinct people, or that their people-consciousness will dissipate at the same speed. It rather alerts us to the fact that the Hakkas today are experiencing a cultural vacuum. Old symbols that have stood for their people-hood for generations, such as hall names, ancestor worship, and Hakka martyrs, are vanishing before new symbols can be found. Modernization brings improvements in material life but offers no answer for spiritual needs. The Hakkas today are standing at a crossroad, in search of new expressions of their peculiar people-hood which they have cherished and depended upon for a sense of security during the long past.

This period of spiritual uncertainty, we believe, is the God-given opportunity for tens of thousands of Hakkas — in small interrelated groups — to move into the eternal security of God's salvation. In another two or three generations, most Hakkas will find themselves in the grip of secularism. Nativistic movements may rise up and claim many Hakka souls. God grant that the church see the urgency on His heart, and act before it is too late!

9

THE CRUCIAL ISSUE OF
ANCESTOR WORSHIP

IN GIVING REASONS for the slow growth of the Hakka church in Taiwan, many Christian spokesmen mentioned the fact that the Hakkas are deeply entrenched in their ancestor worship. This point is often made in such a manner that ancestor worship is held up as another proof for the hopeless resistance of the Hakkas. It is true that ancestor worship has been a great hindrance to the Hakkas becoming Christians, but have we sought to understand what this age-old practice means to them? Have we tried our best to design appropriate ways to deal with it? If not, isn't this another kind of neglect?

The problem of ancestor worship is not limited to the Hakkas. It is a common roadblock against the conversion of all Chinese. In fact, this same problem is affecting the Christianization of hundreds of other peoples throughout the world. The nature and practice of ancestor worship is not the same in Asia, Africa, Oceania, and Latin America, and yet the way it hinders the conversion to Christ is very similar. Let the discussion on Chinese ancestor worship presented in this chapter stimulate our thinking with this crucial issue among other "resistant" peoples.

CHINESE ANCESTOR WORSHIP

The Chinese ancestor worship is by no means a thing of the past. To the great majority of the population in Taiwan — Minnans and Hakkas alike — ancestor worship still occupies an essential position in their religious life. It is a family and clan affair believed to ensure the peace and prosperity of living descendants.

In a recent survey report, a Jesuit priest wrote:

> It is necessary to distinguish carefully the two kinds of spirits that are venerated. The spirit-gods are all connected with popular folklore and associated with needs of the people. But they can be replaced when new spirits catch the fancy of the people or new devotions come into vogue. But not so the ancestor spirits. To destroy the ancestor tablets is the worst possible calamity.[1]

In an anthropological study carried out among the Minnan people at Hsin Hsing village on the west coast of Taiwan, Gallin observed the following regarding Confucianism and ancestor worship:

> The moral and ethical teachings of Confucianism are present in the rules of correct behavior which have been passed down from generation to generation of villagers. Filial piety, respect for age and authority, and worship of the ancestors are all considered both important and fundamental to correct behavior. Aptly expressing a rather general feeling, one villager said, "Everyone knows it's natural to act this way. What other way is there to act?"
>
> Ancestor worship . . . is a form of religious belief to which virtually all Hsin Hsing area villagers adhere. The believers are not, however, in agreement about the effect ancestors have on the lives of their descendants. Many in Hsin Hsing do not agree that ancestors provide positive aid to their descendants, but few would deny the misfortunes that are sure to fall if neglected ancestors vengefully fail to protect their unfilial descendants from the many negative spirits.
>
> Since ancestral spirits live in the other world much as they did in this one, they must be fed, cared for, and propitiated. "If these things are not done, the ancestors will be hungry and dissatisfied and in a sense themselves turn into negative spirits, known as Good Brothers (*hao hsiung-ti*). They then wander about causing trouble for any humans with whom they happen to come into contact."[2]

Generally speaking, all Chinese worship their ancestors in a similar manner, although the importance given to that worship is not always the same. With the Minnans, for instance, favorite gods may sometimes receive more attention than the ancestors do. But with the Hakkas, ancestor worship always takes the top place. It is a practice much harder for them to give up than the worship of other deities.

Hakka Ancestor Worship

The following is a brief description of ancestor worship as practiced by the Hakkas in Taiwan today. The worship is commonly called *Pai Ah-kung-p'o* (worshiping grandparents). The central object of the worship is the ancestral tablet. Shown in figure 9.1 is a family tablet acquired from a Hakka Christian in Taiwan. The main tablet (*A*) is a piece of wood elaborately carved, enshrined in an equally elaborate wooden case (not shown in the picture). Written on this particular tablet are:

1. Hall name *(a)*, written horizontally, which reads: "Nan-Yang Hall."
2. The remark *(b)*, written horizontally: "Enshrined and worshipped by Yang Shang descendants."
3. A eulogistic couplet (*c* and *g*), written vertically, which reads: "Achievements of our ancestors last long and benefit the posterity for many generations. Virtues of our progenitors spread parental love widely among their children like spring sunshine."
4. The main inscription (*e*), written vertically, which reads: "Seat of the spirit of ancestors of all foregoing generations of the Yeh clan."
5. The names of the ancestors of two early generations (*d* and *f*). On this tablet there are the twenty-second and twenty-third generations, numbering from the founder of the clan back on mainland China:

$$\left.\begin{array}{l}\text{Patriarch}\\\text{Matriarch}\end{array}\right\}\text{of the 22nd generation}\left[\begin{array}{l}\text{Names and}\\\text{Posthumous names}\end{array}\right]$$

$$\left.\begin{array}{l}\text{Patriarch}\\\text{Matriarch}\\\text{Matriarch}\end{array}\right\}\text{of the 23rd generation}\left[\begin{array}{l}\text{Names and}\\\text{Posthumous names}\end{array}\right]$$

Fig. 9.1. A Hakka Family Tablet

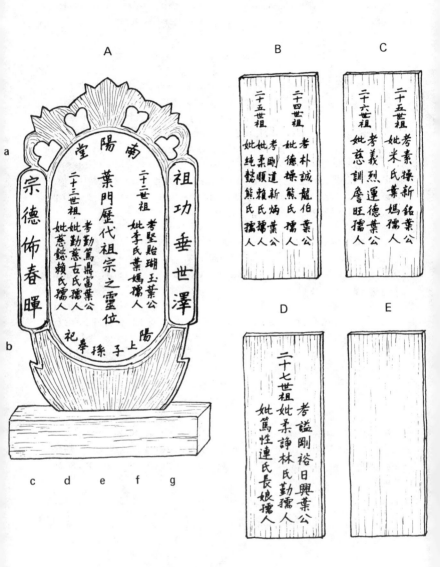

The ancestors of the 22nd generation are probably the first ones migrating to Taiwan from the mainland. There are two matriarchs in the 23rd generation. Most probably these are not plural wives. One must have died before the other was married.

On the back of the tablet, four supplementary plates (*B,C,D,E*) are attached, carrying the names of the ancestors of the succeeding generations:

B. Patriarch ⎫
          ⎬ of the 24th generation   ⎡ Names and ⎤
  Matriarch ⎭   ⎣ Posthumous names ⎦

  Patriarch ⎫
  Matriarch ⎬ of the 25th generation   ⎡ Names and ⎤
  Matriarch ⎭   ⎣ Postnumous names ⎦

C. Patriarch ⎫
          ⎬ of the 25th generation   ⎡ Names and ⎤
  Matriarch ⎭   ⎣ Posthumous names ⎦

  Patriarch ⎫
          ⎬ of the 26th generation   ⎡ Names and ⎤
  Matriarch ⎭   ⎣ Posthumous names ⎦

D. Patriarch ⎫
  Matriarch ⎬ of the 27th generation   ⎡ Names and ⎤
  Matriarch ⎭   ⎣ Posthumous names ⎦

E. [Empty Space]

There are two sets of names for the 25th generation. This means the man of the 26th generation must have been adopted by his sonless uncle (father's brother) in order to carry on the line of descendants. However, he did not want to forget his own father. The empty space on (*E*) is for the 28th generation, the head of the family presently worshiping this tablet.

Each family usually has such a tablet placed on the family altar. Twice a month (lunar), on the first and fifteenth days, the ancestors are worshiped with the offering of food and drink and the burning of incense. On the five or six major festival days throughout the year, a more elaborate worship is conducted. Sacrifice to the ancestors is also made at major events of the family such as engagement, marriage, graduation from school, starting for a long journey, and coming back from it.

Besides family tablets, each lineage has a joint tablet, much larger in size (about 1½ feet wide and 2 feet high), containing the names of more remote ancestors. This tablet is usually kept in the ancestral hall or in the home of the oldest son in the direct line of descent. The routine worship of the joint tablet is performed by the family carrying the responsibility. Once a year on the New Year's day, or twice a year in spring and in autumn, a joint worship is observed in which all families connected with that tablet gather together, each bringing a load of food offerings, to participate in the sacrifice. The form of worship invariably consists of bowing to the tablet, praying, burning incense and paper money, exploding firecrackers, and presenting food and drink offerings.

DIVIDED CHRISTIAN POSITIONS ON ANCESTOR WORSHIP

The amount of difficulty presented by ancestor worship can be seen from the fact that, ever since Christianity came to China, entirely different views and mutually incompatible positions have been held by equally zealous groups of churchmen regarding this matter. Some have advocated nothing less than the total eradication of ancestor worship. By requiring the believers to burn the ancestral tablets and to abstain from all activities connected with the ancestral rites, they have made Christianity to be known as "the ancestor-forsaking religion." Such a frightening image has turned away countless Chinese from the gospel.

Other Christians have doubted if all these difficulties are truly unavoidable. Could it not be that the "worship" is really no more than a civil rite and an Oriental way of showing respect, and not as idolatrous as many have judged it to be? Is there not a more pleasant approach to this notoriously thorny problem? Should not Chinese Christians remember and venerate their ancestors? How should they go about it? These are very interesting questions we want to discuss in this chapter. The attitude of the church toward this crucial issue will have a tremendous bearing on church growth among the Chinese in general, and the Hakkas in particular.

THE EARLY JESUITS AND THE RITES CONTROVERSY

Is Chinese ancestor worship idolatrous? This was the main theme of the historic Rites Controversy (A. D. 1610—1742) which engaged almost the entire Roman Catholic world in a century-long dispute. Matteo (Matthew) Ricci (1552—1610), the first Jesuit missionary to China, was the originator and champion of the view that Chinese ancestor worship was not religious, and therefore should be tolerated by the church.

In his attempt to harmonize Christianity with Chinese culture, which he believed was necessary for Christianity to take root in China, Ricci tried to prove from the Chinese classics that the ancestral rites practiced by the Chinese were only civil in nature. They were ethical rather than religious.

With such an approach, Ricci and his colleagues won favor from the Chinese imperial court, and succeeded in establishing a number of churches in Peking and other cities. Most Jesuits followed Ricci's line and allowed Chinese Catholics to continue the ancestral rites, which the Jesuits believed could be divested of religious meanings by some "corrections." The "corrected" ancestral tablet (fig. 9.2) shows how the Jesuits did this. It is worth minute study. The picture is taken from Dunne with the following explanation:

> Photostat of an early Ch'ing Christian ancestral tablet, the original of which is in the *Bibliothèque National de Paris*. The text within the outline of the cross says: "Worship the true Lord, creator of heaven, earth and all things, and show filial piety to ancestors and parents." The text in the side columns explains the Christian attitude: It is through father and mother that one receives his greatest favors from God. After death, whether they receive punishment or reward, they will not return home. "Therefore," the instruction concludes, "the filial son or kind grandson sets up a tablet or a picture by no means that their spirits might dwell therein, but in order to serve as a reminder of his debt."[3]

But not all Catholic missionaries at that time shared the same view. The Franciscans and Dominicans who entered China in the 1630s were strongly opposed to the Jesuit incorporation of the ancestral rites into the church as designed by Ricci. They believed Chinese ancestor worship was a

Fig. 9.2. A "Corrected" Ancestral Tablet

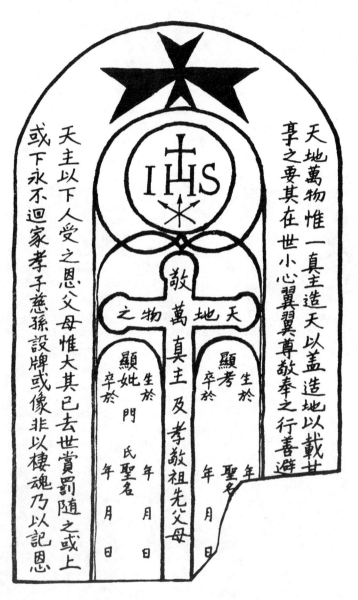

religious act, and therefore an idolatry, which Christianity cannot tolerate at all.

The two sides then entered into prolonged debates, each appealing to the Pope with strong arguments. The controversy lasted well over a hundred years. It was not ended until the Pope finally issued a bull in 1742 condemning the Jesuit position. The Jesuit practice concerning the Chinese rites was thoroughly eradicated from the Catholic church in China.

PROTESTANT POSITIONS ON ANCESTOR WORSHIP

To the Roman Catholics, the papal decrees were the rules to follow; but to the Protestant missionaries who began to enter China early in the nineteenth century, the Bible was the only rule of faith and practice. Ancestor worship still posed a difficult problem with which each of them had to wrestle.

Some argued for the indispensable social functions of the ancestral cult and suggested that it should be purified and preserved. Timothy Richard, the well-known British missionary, was very sympathetic to Ricci's viewpoint. He and a few other Protestant missionaries who held a similar viewpoint by no means advocated tolerance for idolatry. They merely called attention to the importance of the basic Chinese virtue of *hsiao* (filial piety) expressed in the ancestral rites, and were concerned about how the virtue could be preserved without the idolatrous form.

But more were on the other side. They considered ancestor worship downright idolatry, and were inclined to wiping it out at any cost. They pointed out that the Chinese worshiped the ancestors in exactly the same way they worshiped all other deities. The Chinese believed the dead ancestors were truly gods, and must be worshiped and propitiated. It follows naturally that a compromise, in doctrines as well as in forms of worship, is intolerable. By far the majority of Protestant missionaries have taken this position, and many of them have been quite out-spoken about their conviction that ancestor worship should be totally uprooted from the life of Chinese Christians. The following strong statement, for instance, was made by Arthur H. Smith:

> It is a melancholy comment upon the exaggerated Chinese doctrine of piety that it not only embodies no reference to a Supreme Being, but that it does not in any way lead up to a recognition of His existence . . . . It makes dead men into gods, and its only gods are dead men . . . . It has no conception of a Heavenly Father, and feels no interest in such a being when He is made known. Either Christianity will never be introduced into China, or ancestral worship will be given up, for they are contradictories. In the death stuggle between them, the fittest only will survive.[4]

ATTITUDE OF THE CHURCHES IN TAIWAN

More than three centuries have elapsed since the Rites Controversy first erupted; yet the issue of ancestor worship is posing just as much difficulty for the church as it did at that time, and Christian attitudes toward it are just as divided. For a problem which so thoroughly involves the life of hundreds of millions, certainly no simple solution can be expected.

In Taiwan, Roman Catholics are coming back to the position held by Ricci. Yu Pin, Archbishop of Peip'ing (Peking) but currently the president of the Roman Catholic Fu-jen University in Taiwan, was quoted to the effect that

> Taiwan Catholics are going to continue in the line of Li Matou (Matteo Ricci) in the matter of ancestor worship . . . . "If anybody wants to prevent you from performing ceremonies to your ancestors, you come to me. I have the approval of Rome."[5]

During the survey trips made in Taiwan in the fall of 1968, two ministers described to the writer what the Catholic Church did. Their believers are allowed to continue in the ancestral rites, provided the term "shen-wei" (seat of god) on the tablet be changed to "hsiang-wei" (seat of incense), and the offerings, preferably limited to fruit, be first brought to the Catholic priest to be offered to God. During the spring season of worshiping at the graves, Catholic priests take initiative to go to the graves and perform certain ceremonies for the dead. In this way the social life of the people suffers no disruption, and the great offence of Christianity is removed.

The Protestants, on the other hand, have been strongly

united against any tolerance of ancestor worship. This position has been consistently held since the very beginning of Protestant work in Taiwan. What was said by missionaries on the mainland against the ancestral cult is still held to be valid here.

How Shall We Face the Issue?

What, then, is the correct Christian attitude toward the Chinese ancestor worship? The church must face this difficult issue squarely and come up with a definite conclusion. The decision will be chiefly based on the question: Is ancestor worship really religious?

IS ANCESTOR WORSHIP RELIGIOUS?

Modern scholars have found sufficient evidences to show that Chinese ancestor worship as a religion has a very ancient origin.[6] The ancestral cult was already well developed during Shang dynasty (c. 1500—1100 B.C.). One proof of the deification of the dead can be found in the character "heaven"天, which in Chou dynasty (c. 1100—221 B.C.) was written 𣎴, obviously a human figure.[7]

The religious nature of this ancient cult, however, was purposely obscured by a rationalization made by Confucius who reinterpreted the old religion of ancestor worship in terms of its social functions, and advocated its preservation as a support for his socio-ethical system. In order to emphasize the *moral* effect of veneration of ancestors, Confucius deliberately avoided discussion on things supernatural. This Confucianistic view has caused many, especially those among the literati, to deny the religious nature of ancestor worship. The question, therefore, cannot be settled by appeals to the Confucian classics.

In practice, however, the supernatural elements in the ancestral cult have continued to prevail. To the vast majority of Chinese common people, ancestor worship is not only a religion, but the very center of their religious life. The worship involves much more than a filial act, and the tablet is much more than the equivalent of a photo album. Both are a part of idolatry. Neither is a mere symbol of social relationship. Therefore, if there should be a religious change at all, ancestor worship is a main area of the change. It is inconsistent to banish Buddhist and Taoist idolatry and tolerate ancestor worship. It is equally untenable to say that we do not worship the ancestral spirits but will tolerate the tablet — the commonest idol in all China.

The question that faces us now is rather: What is the best way to dissociate ancestor worship and ancestral tablets totally from the life of Chinese Christians?

TRADITIONAL APPROACH TOO NEGATIVE

The chief source of failure in the past, we believe, is the undue emphasis given to the negative side of the change. Abolition of the worship of ancestor and idols has been given so much attention that it appears as if it were the ultimate goal of the Christian gospel, rather than a step toward it. Such an ill-proportioned presentation of Christianity has been detrimental. Christians are known to be, first and foremost, persons who are at great odds with their own ancestors. Even the names of ancestors are not allowed a place in the very house which they have procured for their children. The situation described in the following paragraph is still largely true in Taiwan today:

> The Christian Church in China up to the present time has been using prohibitive measures almost entirely in dealing with the question of ancestor worship. Hence those outside the church have misunderstood and misjudged it. It is the common conception of non-Christians that Christians care nothing for their ancestors, and that one has to abandon one's regard for one's ancestors before he can join the church and be baptized. This is a very wrong conception and is most unfortunate.[8]

Creating such a wrong image of Christianity has made it very difficult for new Christians to bring more of their relatives to Christ. Furthermore, when the negative work has once become the goal, little can be done on the positive side. This tends to leave the new Christian in a cultural vacuum with no help given to him for the readjustment of his relationship to those around him. Frustration in this area has sometimes led to reversion to the old worship.

POSITIVE SIDE TO BE STRENGTHENED

Side by side with the negative should go the positive. The burning of ancestral tablets, for instance, should be seen as a rather inconspicuous part of the great process of *installing a much better way of honoring the ancestors*. The positive side of our work should always overshadow the negative side and fill up the gaps left by the removal of the undesirable things. Both Christians and non-Christians should be brought to realize that the Christian faith far surpasses the ancestral cult in carrying out all its social and psychological functions, and Christianization fulfils rather than condemns, replaces rather than destroys. It should be constantly kept in mind that our goal is to help others readjust their whole life in both spiritual and physical realms, and that to *their* benefit.

Two basic items are needed to perform the positive side of the change: the teaching of the truth, and the skillful use of functional substitutes.

The importance of Christian teaching is demonstrated in the example left by George MacKay, the pioneer missionary in northern Taiwan. When dealing with what he called "the ancestral idolatry," he nevertheless focused the attention on the heavenly Father, and allowed time for the truth to triumph over false beliefs. Said he,

> It has been my custom never to denounce or revile what is so sacredly cherished, but rather to recognize whatever of truth or beauty there is in it, and to utilize it as an "open sesame" to the heart. Many many times, standing on the steps of a temple, after singing a hymn, have I repeated the fifth commandment, and the words "Honor thy father and thy mother" never failed to secure respectful attention. Sometimes a frail old man, whose queue was white, and whose hands trembled on his staff, would nod approvingly and say, "That is heavenly doctrine." Having gained common ground, and having discoursed on the duties to earthly parents, the transition of thought to our Father in heaven is easily made. Prejudices have been overcome in this way, and minds disposed to the truth of the gospel. The worship of idols is first given up; but it may be months—perhaps a year—before the tablet can be forsaken. The truth about the soul, death, and the hereafter must be firmly grasped, or it will wring the heart to throw away the tablet.[9]

Teaching the truth enables people to come to God and receive from Him an abundant life which makes ancestor worship both meaningless and unnecessary. When people know they are secure under the guidance and protection of an all-loving, omnipotent heavenly Father, propitiation of and prayer to the ancestral spirits lose their importance. When Christians truly honor their fathers and mothers according to the scriptural injunction and by the empowering of the Holy Spirit, ancestral rites are no longer needed to teach filial piety and strengthen family ties. Severance from the old religion is seen to be both sensible and natural.

FUNCTIONAL SUBSTITUTES

Functional substitutes, however, help the abundant Christian life express itself visibly among the Christians as well as non-Christians in the context of the local culture. Some concrete patterns of Christian life must be developed so that the positive effect of Christianization can be demonstrated in a culturally relevant way.

Since ancestor worship carries important social functions for the Chinese, the matter of functional substitutes has long been in the mind of Chinese Christians. The practices adopted on the mainland are quite similar to those currently used in Taiwan. Christians have generally disapproved the following forms connected with ancestor worship:

Kneeling and kowtowing before the tablet and casket in the funeral
Burning of incense and paper money at the ancestral shrine
Sacrifices and presenting of sacrificial foods
Burning of candles before the tablet
All idolatrous ceremonies at the grave
Worship of ancestral tablets [10]

Filial piety to living parents (including birthday celebrations) and well-arranged funerals for the dead are the two practices which Chinese Christians have all agreed on as basic duties of Christian children. Chinese Christians usually adopt a Western type funeral ceremony performed by a minister, with only wreaths and an enlarged photograph of the deceased placed in front of the casket. Opportunity is always taken to speak to the nonchristian relatives about the gospel.

The following forms of remembering deceased parents and ancestors are being used in varying degrees by Christians in Taiwan. Some of them are the nonreligious parts of the customary practices, others are Christian substitutes for the idolatrous ceremonies.

1. Ten Commandments, Bible verses, and a picture of Christ. The family altar, situated immediately in front of the central wall in the central hall of each house, is the center of the spiritual life of the nonchristian family. When the family is converted and ancestral tablets and other idols are removed from the altar table, the empty space on the central wall conveys an unbearable sense of spiritual void. It has been a common practice of Taiwan Presbyterian Church, therefore, to hang on the central wall the Ten Commandments and Bible verses written on large sheets of paper and carefully framed. A large picture of Christ is also used.

2. Photographs. An enlarged and framed photograph of the deceased is usually hung in a prominent place in the house, but not on the spot once occupied by the ancestral tablets.

3. Memorial meeting in the home. This takes the place of the routine sacrificial ceremony performed by the non-Christians to the ancestral tablets, although the Christian memorial meeting is much less frequent. Usually it takes place once a year on the anniversaries of the day of death, and the local pastor is asked to preside over it.

4. Visiting and cleaning the graves. This is part of the regular Chinese annual festival *Ch'ing Ming* which occurs on the fifth of April, fifteen days after vernal equinox. Christians go with the crowds to visit and clean the graves, but omit the idolatrous items such as the graveside sacrifices and the burning of paper money. Sometimes the Western custom of placing flowers is used by Christians. Some prefer to do this on another date, say, on the Saturday before Easter Sunday, in order to be separated from the idolatrous connotation of the festival.

5. Fellowship with nonchristian relatives at ancestral

sacrifice gatherings. Some Christians say they continue to go to the annual meetings where people of common lineage come together to offer sacrifices to the ancestors. Christians have nothing to do with the sacrificial offerings. The purpose of their presence is to maintain fellowship with the relatives, and to show them that they have not forsaken the ancestors and the clan people.

6. Family records. Christians are encouraged to prepare their own family records similar to those possessed by the clan leaders. One publisher in Taiwan has made blank forms of family records available for use by Christians. Hakka ministers are especially anxious to get Christians to prepare such records in order to show non-Christians their regard for their glorious ancestry.

7. Memorial gifts. This custom is by no means widely adopted by Christians in Taiwan. On occasion, however, donations in memory of the departed loved ones are given for Christian work or to charity institutions.

These functional substitutes have been used with satisfactory results, but they must be much more widely and consistently practiced by Christians all over the island before a healthy image can be produced of Christianity in the eyes of the Chinese world. More adequate items should be added. The following, to the writer's knowledge, have not been practiced in Taiwan, but appear to have good possibilities.

1. Names of ancestors hung on wall. A veteran Hakka pastor in Taiwan mentioned to the writer that the hardest part of removing ancestral tablets is the sorrow in the Christian's heart at having to deny the beloved progenitors a place in the family. He feared that his children would forget their ancestors. A possible solution for this, he suggested, would be a large, beautiful frame, containing the names and brief descriptions of all the main ancestors, hung at a prominent spot in the house. This is different from the photographs which portray only the most recent generations.

2. Family Bible. This was proposed by two Christian leaders on the mainland.[11] The local pastor should suggest that the new Christian family write the names of all its ancestors on the blank pages provided in a large-size family Bible, which can then be placed in a prominent place such as

on the altar table where the ancestral tablets are usually found.

3. Annual memorial meetings in the church on a special "Ancestor's Day." In such a meeting Christians will be brought to a special remembrance of the past generations, and exhorted to add more honor to the family reputation by achievements in various areas. This has been the practice of some Christians on the mainland.

> The . . . church or churches observe annually a special day as a "Memorial Day." Services are held in the church or at the cemetery in commemoration of the departed parents. Such a day is also observed by individual Christian families where no united effort is made.[12]

Some churches had this kind of meeting on the Spring Festival (presumably the fifth of April) or the Chinese (lunar) New Year's Day to take the place of the customary sacrifices.

> At the Spring Festival one church has its members bring their family records or genealogies to church, and another puts pictures of deceased members on the walls . . . . The Kengchiatsun Church . . . has this unusual Christian custom: Early on the morning of the Lunar New Year the Christians meet for a service and then the family heads of the Keng clan take their families to the ancestral hall and tell them of their ancestors' history.[13]

4. Annual memorial meeting held by Christian members of a clan or an extended family. Nonchristian members may be invited to attend. Besides a Christian service for the memory of ancestors and for the fellowship of living members, the program may include other activities such as an athletic meet or a commendation ceremony for members who have academic or other achievements during the year.

5. Memorial trees. "Some churches plant trees or flowers in the church cemetery at the ancestor worship festival."[14] This is a useful and durable monument for the deceased. Tree planting at the grave side is a traditional Chinese practice. One tree, planted at Confucius' tomb (in Shantung province) by his disciples, is said to be still living today.

6. Family records kept at church. Instead of keeping the family records at home, Christians should be able to store

them in a special foyer in the church. This will strengthen the tie of the church to the families, and make it easier for nonchristian family members to come to church. The church might well fulfill the function of the clan hall.

———————

Surely there is no easy solution for this difficult problem of ancestor worship. Every conversion of an ancestor-worshiper into a God-worshiper is nothing short of a miracle. While we praise God for His wonderful acts in the past, let us be all the more diligent in seeking, under the guidance of the Holy Spirit, new ways and means to give the liberating gospel of Jesus Christ to the millions who have been under the bondage of this age-old religious practice.

10

UNDERSTANDING AND WINNING
EACH "RESISTANT" PEOPLE

IN THIS BOOK we have used the Hakkas in Taiwan to illustrate how the church may neglect a people by ignoring both the difference in culture and the people-consciousness resulting from such a difference. It is our hope and prayer that numerous missionaries and national churchmen in every continent and every civilization will look at their "resistant" peoples in which the church is not prospering, and ask the following questions: Do the people hear the gospel and read the Bible in their own mother tongue? Do they join churches solidly of "our own people"? Does their church leadership come from among themselves? Does Christianity preserve the culture or destroy it? Each of these "resistant" peoples needs to be understood and won by an approach specially directed to it.

But this principle has an even wider application. So far we have been talking about peoples that are easily recognized as being distinctive. Each of them can be distinguished by conspicuous racial or linguistic characteristics. But we all realize that often a society of one race and one language can be further divided into smaller units according to differences in education, customs, life mentality, religious habits, patterns of actions, and choice in marriage. These cultural characteristics are less obvious than the distinctions in race and language, but are no less important.

More often than we like to admit, people are confined to their own little world. This is especially the case in Oriental societies. In order to understand accurately the responsiveness or resistance of any one society, we need to subdivide it into units in which the members of each unit think and live alike, interact with each other frequently, feel perfectly at home in each other's presence, and usually marry among themselves. When we see the society in this way, we will likely discover that these social units are very different from each other in their degree of Christianization. Some units may have a high percentage of Christians, while others have a low percentage. One unit may be a hidden "new tribe" in which the gospel has never been effectively proclaimed. Another unit may never have had a missionary living in its bounds. Members of one unit may have to work seven days a week so they never dreamed they could become Christians. Members of another unit may find that the Bible, though available in their language, is written in a style far above their heads, or printed in a foreign script which they cannot read. If the church is not making progress in some of these units, is it because they are resistant—or simply neglected?

Each of these social units should really be considered a distinctive people. Each of them, too, needs to be understood and won by an approach that is specially directed to it.

God's plan will not be fully consummated until men and women are redeemed by the blood of the Lamb out of *every kindred, every tongue, every people, every nation.* Let us give ourselves diligently to God for the task of winning the hundreds of *peoples* in the world who look resistant—but are being neglected.

APPENDIX A
PROTESTANTS IN TAIWAN
(1967)

Denominations	Communicant Member ship*	Community Size (estimated)†				
		Minnan	Hakka‡	Main-lander	High-lander	Total
Taiwan Presbyterian Church	70,407	83,591	2,800	1,000	77,583	164,974
Church Assemblies (Little Flock)	30,000	6,000		54,000		60,000
True Jesus Church (Indigenous Pentecostal)	22,000	21,160	840		22,000	44,000
Southern Baptist Church	9,363	1,860	140	16,700		18,700
Seventh-Day Adventist Church	4,965	3,000		3,000	3,900	9,900
Taiwan Lutheran Church	3,488	700		6,300		7,000
Methodist Church	3,255	650		5,850		6,500
Taiwan Holiness Church	3,000	5,000		200	800	6,000
"Local Church"	2,840	570		5,130		5,700
Other Foreign-mission-related Churches (34 Groups)	21,406	6,500	820	34,480	1,000	42,800
Independent Churches	7,041	7,700		6,400		14,100
Total (approximately)	178,000	137,000	5,000	133,000	105,000	380,000
Protestant Percentage in the Population of Each Group		1.4%	0.3%	10.1%	33.3%	average: 2.9%

* Figures from *Taiwan Christian Yearbook* (1968).

† Except when exact data are available as in the case of Taiwan Presbyterian Church, community size is taken as two times communicant membership. The further breakdown into ethno-cultural groups represents largely my own estimation.

‡ This does not include Hakka members in Minnan or Mandarin churches.

APPENDIX B

COMPOSITION OF TAIWAN POPULATION IN 1956

(With Extrapolation for 1967)

Administrative Division	Taiwanese		Highlander	Mainlander	Others ‡	Total
	Of Fukien Ancestry*	Of Kuangtung Ancestry†				
Taipei County	564,635	14,617	1,192	86,568	1,081	668,093
Yilan County	268,050	7,243	6,697	20,871	327	303,188
Taoyuan County	194,453	181,135	6,316	29,464	207	411,575
Hsinchu County	124,153	236,156	8,910	39,483	351	409,053
Miaoli County	111,413	264,530	6,388	12,442	551	395,324
Taichung County	415,608	99,003	2,142	20,369	265	537,387
Changhua County	750,682	28,342	11	14,068	755	793,858
Nantou County	288,375	46,664	13,913	8,015	317	357,284
Yunlin County	581,235	13,450	70	9,445	284	604,484
Chiayi County	569,842	28,557	2,323	29,351	309	630,382
Tainan County	682,323	4,182	6,201	15,268	237	708,211
Kaohsiung County	422,033	61,864	9,150	41,243	379	534,669
Pingtung County	373,263	114,697	38,331	41,640	538	568,469
Taitung County	72,844	23,486	59,287	13,954	256	169,827
Hualien County	77,498	55,701	60,202	26,026	274	219,701

Penghu County	80,092	101	8	5,650	35	85,886
Keelung City	136,548	4,198	92	52,579	589	194,006
Taipei City	499,860	28,933	247	291,838	2,590	823,468
Taichung City	190,610	10,578	90	45,411	399	247,088
Tainan City	240,762	1,530	41	41,255	612	284,200
Kaohsiung City	269,312	11,383	163	83,339	962	365,159
Islandwide Population (1956)	6,913,591	1,236,350	221,774	928,279	11,318	9,311,312
Percentage	74.25%	13.28%	2.38%	9.97%	0.12%	100.00%
Islandwide Population (1967) (extrapolated)	9,835,000	1,759,000	315,000	1,321,000	16,000	13,246,000§

SOURCE: Taiwan Provincial Government (1956 General Census).

*Taken as Minnans.

†Taken as Hakkas.

‡Including foreigners and non-Highland Taiwanese with an ancestry other than Fukien or Kuangtung.

§Total population in 1967 (*China Yearbook* 1968). This total is broken down into the five groups by using 1956 percentages.

HAKKA SONGS AND FOLKLORE

The following three songs and their English translations are taken from **China Review** (1884a:507, 508; 1884b:20). (Mandarin transliterations are mine.) It is to be noted that the same kind of songs are still being sung by the Hakkas today.

Ah-mei sheng-ch'eng feng-huang sheng
Chao-jih tan-ts'ai shou k'u-hsing
Chao-chih chin-jih ch'iung nan-kuo
Ho-pu tang-ch'u chia hao-jen

My lass, your form is like that of the phoenix:
It is indeed hard work for you to carry fuel all the day.
If you had known betimes what hardships were in store for you,
I think you would have married a better man.

Sung lang sung-tao ta-men ch'ien
Chu-fu cha-lang chi-chu yen
Chih-chu cha-lang san-chien shih
Chieh-chiu ch'u-hua mo-tu-ch'ien

I escort my lad, I escort him to the front door,
And I give my lad a few words of advice:
Three matters I impress strongly upon my lad:
"Avoid wine, eschew women, and do not gamble."

Sung lang sung-tao shih-li-t'ing
Tsai sung shih-li nan-she-ch'ing
Tsai sung shih-li ch'ing-nan-she
Shin-feng nan-she yu-ch'ing-jen

I escort my lad, I escort him to the three-mile post:
Another three miles for it is hard to part:
Still another three for parting is hard:
Hard it is indeed to part from a lover.

This contemporary song is found in Hsieh (1965:6:55). (Translation is mine.)

Kuo-lai Hualien shih-chi-nien
Chien-nan hsing-k'u wu-ts'ang-ch'ien
Jen shuo Tung-pu ch'ien hao-chuan
Chuan-ch'ien chien-hsing k'u nan-yen

Well over ten years have I come over to Hualien,
    In difficulties and hard work I have accumulated no fortune.
Everybody says making money is easy on the east coast,
    But really it is with such hardship which no mere words can describe.

The following bit of folklore was taken from a Hakka ballad (my translation).

THE STORY OF YELLOW RATTAN

Huang Ts'ao was a sharp student in Chinese classics, but he was as ugly as a devil. That year he went up to Peking to take the court examination. He would have won the top place, but the foolish Emperor turned him down because he was too ugly. Huang Ts'ao was so angry that he swore he would kill people in the unjust world. He brought a hundred thousand men with him and killed right and left through the provinces. Some people went all the way to southern Kiangsi to escape him. When they happened to climb up a rocky mountain toward the east, they found a long and deep valley. They went into the rocky valley, and discovered a small village inside. Upon inquiring they learned this was Ning-hua county, T'ingchou prefecture, Fukien province. The name of the village was Shih-pi (stone wall).

Now when Huang Ts'ao marched with his ferocious soldiers after the refugees, he happened to notice a poor woman running for her life. On her back she carried a big boy, and dragged in her hand was a little one trotting by her side. Huang Ts'ao was surprised. He asked: "Excuse me, lady, may I ask why you carry the big boy instead of the little one?" Without knowing this was the Great Rebel himself, the woman answered, "Sir, run quick for your life. Huang Ts'ao is coming. The big boy I am carrying is my husband's brother's son. His parents were just killed, and he is the only descendant in that family line. He must not die. As to the little one, he is my own son."

Even Huang Ts'ao could not let such a good heart be killed. He said, "Don't be afraid, lady. When you get to a house, just hang up a string of yellow rattan on the door post, and you'll be all right."

Strict order went through Huang Ts'ao's army that nobody was to touch the house with yellow rattan on it. The woman happened to run to the Shih-pi (stone wall) village. She hurried to tell the people there to hang up a lot of yellow rattan on the stone gate of that valley, and so the whole village was spared. Those people were the ancestors of us Hakkas.

FIELD SURVEY FORMS

Questionnaire A

(Sent to all churches in areas having 20% or more Hakka population)

1. Are there Hakka Christians in your congregation?

2. Facts about your church:

   1) When established?
   2) Language(s) used in church meetings?
   3) Version of Bible used in church meetings?
   4) Version of hymn book used in church meetings?
   5) Is the minister of the church a Hakka?
   6) Does the minister preach in Hakka?
   7) Membership figures:

      Total households   ____ How many Hakka ____
      Total communicants   ____ How many Hakka ____
      Total non-communicants ____ How many Hakka ____

3. Facts about your area (village or town):

   1) Percentage of Hakka population
   2) Particular customs and religious practices of the Hakka people in your area
   3) The Work of the Roman Catholic Church in your area

4. Your opinions about Hakka work:

   1) What are the main difficulties and hindrances in Hakka work?
   2) Do the Hakkas in your area show signs of responsiveness?
   3) What policies and methods should be adopted in order to effect greater church growth in Hakka areas?

    4) What do you think of the suggestion that more Hakka-speaking churches should be established?

    5) Other opinions or suggestions

Schedule B

(For interview with ministers and missionaries)

1. How was your church planted?

2. Does your church major in Hakka work? Why?

3. Who are your Hakka members?

    Occupation
    New Christians or Christians by inheritance?
    Adults (men or women) or young people?

4. In your opinion, why is church growth in Hakka areas difficult?

    Objective factors having to do with Hakka peculiarities
    Subjective factors having to do with policies, approaches, and methods adopted by the Church
    What are some of the weaknesses of our current evangelism among the Hakkas?

5. How can we win the Hakkas more effectively?
    Is there a future for Hakka church growth?
    If so, how should we go about it?

Schedule C

(For interview with Hakka converts)

1. Are you a local resident? Or did you move from other parts of Taiwan?

2. How did you become a Christian?
   Inherited from parents?
   Who led you to Christ?
   Did some of your relatives also become Christians?

3. What was the motive of your becoming a Christian?

4. Did you worship ancestors before you became a Christian? If so, how?

5. Did you stop ancestor worship immediately after you became a Christian?

6. What did you do with the ancestral tablet?

7. What was the reaction of your parents, relatives, and neighbors when they knew you no longer worshiped ancestors?

8. Has your relationship with them changed considerably?

9. Have you brought any of your relatives to Christ since you became a Christian? If you feel this difficult, explain why.

NOTES

CHAPTER 3 *(Pages 24-38)*

1. Marshall Broomhall, *The Chinese Empire*, p. 394.
2. Wilhelm Oehler, "Christian Work Among the Hakka," in *The Christian Occupation of China*, ed. M.T. Stauffer, p. 352.
3. D. MacGillivray, *A Century of Protestant Missions in China*, p. 474.
4. Ibid., p. 476.
5. Ibid., pp. 477-78, 480.
6. Ibid., pp. 477-79.
7. Wilhelm Oehler, *China und die christliche Mission in Geschichte und Gegenwart*. p. 263.
8. MacGillivray, p. 482.
9. Ibid., pp. 480, 482.
10. Oehler, "Christian Work," p. 353.
11. MacGillivray, pp. 175, 179, 181, 183-84, 188, 197-98.
12. W. Bernard Paton, *The "Strange People,"* pp. 35-37.
13. Ibid., pp. 52-54.
14. MacGillivray, pp. 484-89.
15. Oehler, "Christian Work," pp. 352-53.
16. Ibid., p. 353.
17. MacGillivray, p. 6.
18. Ibid., p. 314.
18a. Oehler, p. 353.
19. Broomhall, p. 394.
20. Oehler, "Christian Work," p. 351.
20a. Broomhall, p. 99.
21. Edward H. Parker, "Syllabary of the Hakka Language or Dialect," *China Review* 8:205-17.
22. Oehler, "Christian Work," p. 351.
23. John F. Donovan, *The Pagoda and the Cross*, p. 75.
24. Ibid.
25. Ibid., pp. 67-68.
26. Ibid., pp. 76, 81.
27. Ibid., pp. 79-80.
28. Ibid., pp. 89-90, 94.
29. Ibid., pp. 85-86, 113, 121.
30. Ibid., pp. 87-88, 116, 119-20.
31. *Catholic Directory of Taiwan*, pp. 8-10.
32. Hollington K. Tong, *Christianity in Taiwan: A History*, p. 221.
33. *Catholic Directory of Taiwan*, p. 374.

CHAPTER 4 *(Pages 39-54)*

1. Edward Band, *Barclay of Formosa*, pp. 61-66.
2. Ibid., p. 66.
3. George L. MacKay, *From Far Formosa*, pp. 156-57.
4. James H. Taylor, Sr., ed., *Entering the Open Door in Formosa*, pp. 63-67.
5. MacKay, p. 157.

6. Ibid.
7. Ibid., pp. 175-78.
8. Ibid.
9. Ch'ien-hsin Hsu and Lien-ming Cheng, eds., *Taiwan Chi-tu Chang-lao Chiao-hui Pai-nien-shih* (A Centennial History of Taiwan Presbyterian Church, 1865-1965), pp. 47-49.
10. Duncan MacLeod, *The Island Beautiful,* p. 122.
11. William Campbell, *Missionary Success in the Island of Formosa.* 2:442-43.
12. Ibid., pp. 445-46.
13. Ibid.
14. Ibid., pp. 431-32.
15. Hsu and Cheng, p. 105.

CHAPTER 5 *(Pages 55-68)*

1. William Campbell, *Sketches from Formosa,* pp. 249-50.
2. Duncan MacLeod, *The Island Beautiful,* p. 227. Italics added.
3. *Catholic Directory of Taiwan,* pp. 377-79.
4. George L. MacKay, *From Far Formosa,* p. 102. Italics added.
5. Hugh MacMillan, *First Century in Formosa,* p. 120.

CHAPTER 6 *(Pages 69-82)*

1. George Campbell, "Origin and Migration of the Hakkas," *The Chinese Recorder and Missionary Journal* 43:476, 480.
2. Bishop Francis Ford, as cited in John F. Donovan, *The Pagoda and the Cross,* p. 71.
3. Demetrius C. Boulger, *China,* p. 319.
4. James W. Davidson, *The Island of Formosa,* p. 8.
5. Chiao-min Hsieh, *Taiwan   Ilha Formosa,* p. 150.
6. W. G. Goddard, *Formosa: A Study in Chinese History,* pp. xiii-xiv, 24.
7. *Encyclopedia Britannica* 11 (1962):87.
8. E. J. Eitel, "Ethnographical Sketches of the Hakka Chinese," in *Notes and Queries on China and Japan,* p. 65.
9. Campbell, pp. 474-75.
10. Rudolf Lechler, "The Hakka Chinese," *The Chinese Recorder and Missionary Journal* 9:353-54.
11. Campbell, p. 475.
12. C. P. Fitzgerald, *China: A Short Cultural History,* pp. 378-79.
13. T'ai-P'ing-huan-yu-chi, as cited in T'ing-yu Hsieh, "Origin and Migration of the Hakkas," *Chinese Social and Political Science Review* 13:211.
14. Yu-ti-chi-sheng, as cited in Ibid.
15. Campbell, p. 479.
16. Lechler, pp. 353-54.
17. Hsiang-lin Lo, *K'eh-chia Shih-liao Hui-pian* (Historical Sources for the Study of the Hakkas).
18. Shou-hua Kuo, *K'eh-chia Yuan-liu Hsin-chih* (History of Hakka Chinese), pp. 62-64.

19. Milton T. Stauffer, ed., *The Christian Occupation of China*, pp. 7, 8, 158.
20. Eitel, p. 65.
21. W. D. MacIver, *An English-Chinese Dictionary in the Vernacular of the Hakka People in the Canton Province*, p. v.
22. Robert A. D. Forrest, *The Chinese Language*, p. 236.

CHAPTER 7 *(Pages 83-97)*

1. George Campbell, "Origin and Migration of the Hakkas," *The Chinese Recorder and Missionary Journal* 43:479.
2. Wilhelm Oehler, "Christian Work Among the Hakka," in *The Christian Occupation of China*, ed. M. T. S. Stauffer, p. 351.
3. Campbell, p. 474.
4. Shu-hsin Hsieh, ed. *Chung-yuan Wen-hua Ts'ung-shu* (Symposium on Chung-yuan Cultures), 1:1-12.
5. Oehler, p. 351.
6. Rudolf Lechler, "The Hakka Chinese," *The Chinese Recorder and Missionary Journal* 9:355.
7. T'ing-yu Hsieh, "Origin and Migration of the Hakkas," *Chinese Social and Political Science Review* 13:222.
8. Archibald Little, *The Far East*, p. 137.
9. Robert A. D. Forrest, *The Chinese Language*, p. 237.
10. Mr. Spiker, as cited in Ellsworth Huntington, *The Character of Races*, p. 168.
11. Campbell, p. 473.
12. Vincent Y. C. Shih, *The Taiping Ideology*, pp. 308-9.
13. Huntington, p. 168.
14. Lechler, p. 357.
15. E. J. Eitel, "Ethnographical Sketches of the Hakka Chinese," in *Notes and Queries on China and Japan*, 1:114.
16. Eitel, "Hakka Literature," in *Notes and Queries on China and Japan*, 1:113.
17. Eitel, "Ethnographical Sketches," 1:113.

CHAPTER 8 *(Pages 98-116)*

1. Rudolf Lechler, "The Hakka Chinese," *The Chinese Recorder and Missionary Journal* 9:358.
2. F. Hubrig, "Ueber die Hakka-Chinesen," *Verhandlunger der Berliner Gesellschaft fuer Anthropologie, Ethnologie und Urgeschichte* 11:105.
3. See A. C. Krass, "A Case Study in Effective Evangelism in West Africa," *Church Growth Bulletin*, vol. 4, no. 1.
4. Donald A. McGavran, *Understanding Church Growth*, pp. 200-201.
5. Margaret Mead, ed., *Cultural Patterns and Technological Change*, pp. 293-94.
6. Eugene A. Nida, "Akamba Initiation Rites and Culture Themes," *Practical Anthropology* 9:155.
7. McGavran, p. 211.

8. "A Separate Path to Equality," *Life* 65 (Dec. 13, 1968):84.
9. Mead, p. 67.
10. Ibid., p. 117.
11. Ibid., p. 183.
12. Ibid., p. 292.
13. McGavran, p. 213.
14. Ibid., pp. 298-299.
15. Ibid., pp. 297-298, 303.
16. *Christian Tribune,* Dec. 22, 1968, p. 6.
17. McGavran, *The Bridges of God,* p. 129.

CHAPTER 9 *(Pages 117-134)*

1. Robert J. Ronald, "Religion on Taiwan: A Survey Report," p. 22.
2. Bernard Gallin, *Hsin Hsing. Taiwan: A Chinese Village in Change.* pp. 232-34.
3. George H. Dunne, *Generation of Giants.* p. 293.
4. Arthur H. Smith, *Chinese Characteristics.* p. 185.
5. Lien-Hua Chow, "The Problem of Funeral Rites." *Practical Anthropology* 11 (1964):227.
6. Herrlee G. Creel, *The Birth of China.* p. 174.
7. Ibid., p. 342.
8. *China Christian Yearbook 1917.* p. 296.
9. George L. McKay, *From Far Formosa.* p. 133.
10. Frank W. Price, *The Rural Church in China.* p. 203.
11. H. R. Williamson, *British Baptists in China.* p. 295.
12. *China Christian Yearbook 1917.* p. 297.
13. Price, pp. 203-4.
14. Ibid., p. 203.

BIBLIOGRAPHY

Sources of Direct References

BAND, Edward
 1936   *Barclay of Formosa.*
         Tokyo: Christian Literature Society.
BOULGER, Demetrius C.
 1898   *China.*
         New York: Peter Fenelon Collier.
BROOMHALL, Marshall
 1907   *The Chinese Empire.*
         London: Morgan & Scott.
 1934   *The Bible in China.*
         London: British and Foreign Bible Society.
CAMPBELL, George
 1912   "Origin and Migration of the Hakkas," *The Chinese Recorder and Missionary Journal,* vol. 43, pp. 473-480. Shanghai, China.
CAMPBELL, William
 1889   *Missionary Success in the Island of Formosa* (vol. 2).
         London: Trubner & Co.
 1915   *Sketches from Formosa.*
         London: Marshall Brothers Ltd.
Catholic Directory of Taiwan.
 1967   Taipei, Taiwan: Hua Ming Press.
China Christian Yearbook 1917.
 1917   Shanghai: Christian Literature Society.
China Christian Yearbook 1934-35.
 1935   Shanghai: Christian Literature Society.
The China Review.
 1884a   "Hakka Songs," vol. 12, no. 6.
 1884b   "Hakka Songs," vol. 13, no. 1.
China Yearbook 1967-68.
 1968   Taipei, Taiwan: China Publishing Co.
CHOW Lien-Hua
 1964   "The Problem of Funeral Rites," *Practical Anthropology,* 11:226-28. (Reprinted from *Quarterly Notes on Christianity & Chinese Religion,* Series 7, no. 2, July 1963, Hong Kong.)

Christian Tribune (Chi-tu-chiao Lun-t'an).
  1968   (A weekly church newspaper, issue of December 22, 1968.) Taipei, Taiwan.
Chung-kuo-shih-pao (China Times).
  1968   (A daily newspaper, issue of September 25, 1968, page 7.) Taipei, Taiwan.

CHUNG Tze-shih
  1965   *Hsuan-chiao Ti-erh Shih-chi Chi-pen Fang-an chi Yen-t'ao Tze-liao (Basic Plans and Study Materials for the Second Century of the Mission).* Taipei, Taiwan: Taiwan Presbyterian Church.

CREEL, Herrlee G.
  1961   *The Birth of China.*
          New York: Frederick Ungar Publishing Co.
DAVIDSON, James W.
  1903   *The Island of Formosa.*
          (Reprinted by Wen-hsing Book House, Taipei, Taiwan.)
DONOVAN, John F.
  1967   *The Pagoda and the Cross.*
          New York: Charles Scribner's Sons.
DUNNE, George H.
  1962   *Generation of Giants.*
          Notre Dame, Ind.: University of Notre Dame Press.
EITEL, E.J.
  1867a   "Hakka Literature," *Notes and Queries on China and Japan,* vol. 1, no. 4, pp. 37-40.
  1867b   "Ethnographical Sketches of the Hakka Chinese,"
          Notes and Queries on China and Japan, vol, 1, nos. 5-12, pp. 49-50, 65-67, 81-83, 97-99, 113-114, 129-130, 145-146, 161-163.
Encyclopaedia Britannica.
  1962   Vol. 11, p. 87.
          Chicago: William Benton.
FITZGERALD, C.P.
  1961   *China: A Short Cultural History.* New York & Washington: Frederick A. Praiger, Publishers.
FORREST, Robert A.D.
  1965   *The Chinese Language.*
          London: Faber & Faber.

GALLIN, Bernard
  1966   *Hsin Hsing, Taiwan: A Chinese Village in Change.*
          Berkeley & Los Angeles: University of California Press.
GODDARD, W. G.
  1966   *Formosa: A Study in Chinese History.* East Lansing, Mich.: Michigan State Univesity Press.
The Hakka Hymnal (K'eh-chia Sheng-ke).
  1967   Taipei, Taiwan: The True Light Publishers.
HSIEH Chiao-min
  1964   *Taiwan—Ilha Formosa.*
          Washington: Butterworths.
HSIEH Shu-hsin, ed.
  1967   *Chung-yuan Wen-hua Ts'ung-shu (Symposium on Chung-yuan Cultures),* vol. 2.
          Miaoli, Taiwan: Chung-yuan & Miao-yu Magazine.
HSIEH T'ing-yu
  1929   "Origin and Migration of the Hakkas," *Chinese Social and Political Science Review,* vol. 13, no. 2, pp. 202-27. Peiping, China.
HSU Ch'ien-hsin and CHENG Lien-ming, eds.
  1965   *Taiwan Chi-tu Chang-lao Chiao-hui Pai-nien-shih (A Centennial History of Taiwan Presbyterian Church, 1865-1965).* Taipei, Taiwan: Taiwan Presbyterian Church.
HUBRIG, F.
  1879   "Ueber die Hakka-Chinesen," *Verhandlunger der Berliner Gesellschaft fuer Anthropologie, Ethnologie und Urgeschichte,* vol. 11, pp. 99-105.
HUNTINGTON, Ellsworth
  1924   *The Character of Races.*
          New York: Charles Scribner's Sons.
KRASS, A.C.
  1967   "A Case Study in Effective Evangelism in West Africa," *Church Growth Bulletin,* vol. 4, no. 1.
KUO Shou-hua
  1964   *K'eh-chia Yuan-liu Hsin-chih (History of Hakka Chinese).* Taipei, Taiwan: Chung-yang Wen-wu Kung-in-she.
LECHLER, Rudolf
  1878   *"The Hakka Chinese,"* The Chinese Recorder and Missionary Journal, vol. 9, no. 5, pp. 352-59.

Life   "A Separate Path to Equality," *Life* weekly, vol.
  1968   65, no. 24, December 13, 1968, pp. 82-98.
          Chicago.

LITTLE, Archibald
  1905   *The Far East.*
          Oxford: Clarendon Press.

McGAVRAN, Donald A.
  1955   *The Bridges of God.*
          London: World Dominion Press.
  1970   *Understanding Church Growth.* Grand Rapids,
          Mich.: Eerdmans.

Mac GILLIVRAY, D.
  1907   *A Century of Protestant Missions in China.*
          Shanghai: American Tract Society.

MacIVER, D.
  1905   *An English-Chinese Dictionary in the Vernacular*
          of the Hakka People in the Canton Province.
          Shanghai: American Presbyterian Mission
          Press.
  1909   *A Hakka Syllabary.*
          Shanghai: Presbyterian Mission Press.

MacKAY, George L.
  1896   *From Far Formosa.*
          New York: Fleming H. Revell Co.

MacLEOD, Duncan
  1923   *The Island Beautiful.*
          Toronto: Board of Foreign Missions of the
          Canadian Presbyterian Church.

MacMILLAN, Hugh
  1963   *First Century in Formosa.*
          Taipei, Taiwan: China Sunday School
          Association.
          (First edition, 1953; Second edition, 1963.)

MEAD, Margaret, ed.
  1955   *Cultural Patterns and Technical Change.* New
          York: United Nations Educational, Scientific,
          and Cultural Organization.

NIDA, Eugene A.
  1962   "Akamba Initiation Rites and Culture Themes,"
          Practical Anthropology, vol. 9, pp. 145-50, 153-
          55.

OEHLER, Wilhelm
   1922   "Christian Work among the Hakka," *The
           Christian Occupation of China*, pp. 351-53, edited
           by M. T. Stauffer.
   1925   *China und die christliche Mission in Geschichte
           und Gengenwart*. Stuttgart: Evangelischer Mis-
           sionverlag G.m.b.H.
PARKER, Edward H.
   1879   "Syllabary of the Hakka Language or Dialect,"
           China Review, vol. 8, pp. 205-17.
PATON, W. Bernard
   n.d.   *The "Stranger People"*. (ca. 1924 or later.)
           London: The Religious Tract Society.
PRICE, Frank W.
   1948   *The Rural Church in China*. New York:
           Agricultural Missions, Inc.
RONALD, Robert J.
   1967   "Religion on Taiwan: A Survey Report." (A
           mimeographed paper.) Hsinchu, Taiwan.
SHIH, Vincent Y. C.
   1967   *The Taiping Ideology*.   Seattle and London:
           University of Washington Press.
SMITH, Arthur H.
   1894   *Chinese Characteristics*. New York: Fleming H.
           Revell.
STAUFFER, Milton T., ed.
   1922   *The Christian Occupation of China*. Shanghai:
           China Continuation Committee.
Taiwan Christian Yearbook 1968
   1968   Taipei, Taiwan: Taiwan Missionary Fellowship.
Taiwan Presbyterian Church
   1949-   *Taiwan Chiao-hui Kung-pao (Taiwan Church
   1968   Bulletin)*.
   1958-   "K'eh-chuang Hsuan-tao-hui Yi-shih-lu" (Minutes
   1965   of Hakka Evangelism Board).
   1958-   "Tsung-hui T'ung-ch'ang Hui-yi Yi-shih-lu"
   1968   (Minutes of General Assembly Meetings).
   1965   "Into a New Era Together." (A mimeograed
           paper.)
   1966   *Tsung-hui Nien-chien (The Church Yearbook)*.
Taiwan Provincial Government
   1958   *Chung-hua-min-kuo Hu-k'ou P'u-ch'a Pao-kao-
           shu (Report on 1956 General Census of the Re-
           public of China)*.

TAYLOR, James H., Sr., ed.
    1956   *Entering the Open Door in Formosa.* Winona
            Lake, Ind.: Free Methodist Church—
            Woman's Missionary Society.
TONG, Hollington K.
    1961   *Christianity in Taiwan: A History.* Taipei,
            Taiwan: by the author.
WILLIAMSON, H. R.
    1957   *British Baptists in China.* London: Carey
            Kingsgate Press.

OTHER SOURCES OF INFORMATION

Many other works, though not directly referred to in this book, have been relied upon for basic information regarding the Hakka people, Christianity among the Hakkas, or the Chinese ancestor worship. Following is only a selected list:

CAMPBELL, William
    1889   *Missionary Success in the Island of Formosa (vol.
            1).* London: Trubner & Co.
CHANG Feng-ch'ien
    1960   *K'eh-chia Min-feng Min-shu chih Yen-chiu (A
            Study on Hakka Customs).* Taipei, Taiwan:
            T'ai-ching Chu'u-pan-she.
CHENG Lien-teh, WU Ch'ing-yi, HSU Ch'ien-shin, CHENG
    1962   Lien-ming *Taiwan Chi-tu Chang-lao Chiao-hui
            Pei-pu Chiao-hui Chiu-shih Chou-nien Chien-shi
            (A Short History of The Northern Churches
            of Taiwan Presbyterian Church).*
            Taipei, Taiwan: Taiwan Presbyterian Church.
EITEL, E. J.
    1868   "Ethnographical Sketches of the Hakka Chinese
            (continued)," *Notes and Queries on China and
            Japan,* vol. 2, nos. 10-11, pp. 145-47, 167-69.
    1869   "Ethnographical Sketches of the Hakka Chinese
            (continued)," *Notes and Queries on China and
            Japan,* vol. 3, no. 1, pp. 1-3.
HSIEH Shu-hsin, ed.
    1965   *Chung-yuan Wen-hua Ts'ung-shu (Symposium on
            Chung-yuan Cultures),* vol. 1.
            Miaoli, Taiwan: Chung-yuan & Miao-yu
            Magazine.

LATOURETTE, Kenneth S.
  1929   *A History of Christian Missions in China.* London: Society for Promoting Christian Knowledge.
LAUFER, Berthold
  1913   "The Development of Ancestral Images in China," *Journal of Religious Psychology,* vol. 6 (1913), pp. 111-23.
LEVESQUE, Leonard
  1967   *Croyances et Coutumes Hakkas.* Kuanhsi, Hsinchu, Taiwan: by the author.
LIAO Yu-wen
  1966   *Taiwan Sheng-hua (Taiwan Mythology).* Taipei, Taiwan: Sheng-sheng Ch'u-pan-she.
LO Hsiang-lin
  1933   *K'eh-chia Yen-chiu Tao-lun (An Introduction to the Study of the Hakkas).*
          Canton, China.

> NOTE: Mr. Lo Hsiang-lin, currently professor of Chinese at the University of Hong Kong, is the only recognized authority on Hakka studies. This book, now out of print, represents his careful academic work on the history of the Hakkas. A Japanese translation which Mr. Lo sent to the writer in 1968, was published in 1942 in Taiwan, apparently by the Japanese government then ruling the island. Much of the materials contained in HSIEH (1965 and 1967) and KUO (1964) are based on this book. Mr. Lo, himself a Hakka, has written extensively on the Hakka people.

  1965   *K'eh-chia Shih-liao Hui-pian (Historical Sources for the Study of the Hakkas).*
          Hong Kong: Chung-kuo Hsiueh-she (Institute of Chinese Culture).
ROWBOTHAM, Arnold H.
  1966   *Missionary and Mandarin.* New York: Russell & Russell.
YANG, C. K.
  1967   *Religion in Chinese Society.* Berkeley & Los Angeles: University of California Press.

INDEX

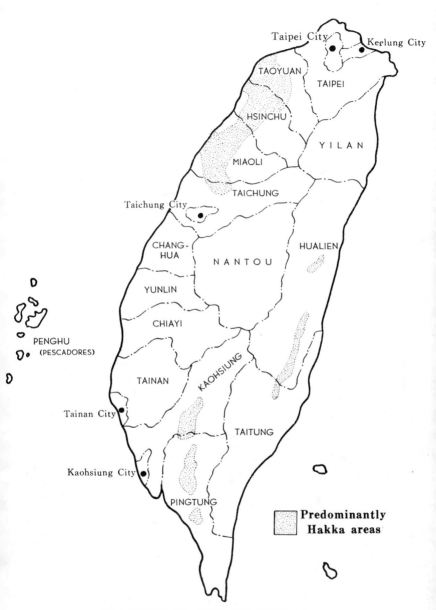

TAIWAN (FORMOSA)
Showing Countries and Large Cities

"HAKKALAND"

Showing Places Mentioned in This Book

HUNAN

KIANGSI

FUKIEN

• Ning-hua
(Nenfa)

Shih-pi •

T'ingchou

• Lien-ch'eng

○ Shang-hang

Chiao-ling
(Cheng-p'ing) ○
| Shou-hang

★ Ta-p'u
|
•Sam-lo

Hsing-ning •
Ch'ang-loh •

Kaying
(Moichu) ★

KUANGTUNG

Lung-ch'uan •

• Jau-p'ing

○ Ying-tak

Ch'aochou •

Ts'ing-yuan ○

○
Hua-hsien

Pok-lo
(Poh-lo)

Wukingfu

Swatow

Canton ●

San-on
(Sin-an)

Huichou
(Kui-shan)
Hai-feng •

Lu-feng

Hoh-san ○

Ch'ih-ch'i ○

Macao

Lilong
Pukak
Kowloon

Hong Kong

Kaying prefecture
(Old Hakkaland)

**Predominantly
Hakka areas**

*Modern name of this chief city of Kaying prefecture is *Mei-hsien*.

NORTHERN AND SOUTHERN TAIWAN
Showing Places Mentioned in This Book

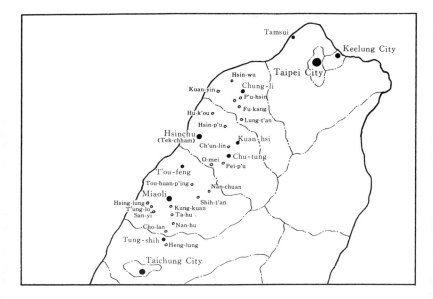

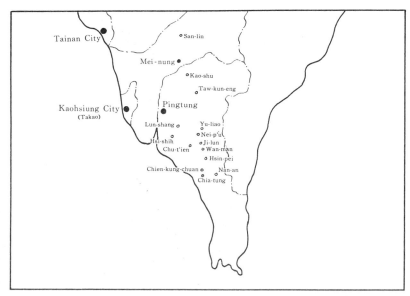

CHINA
Showing Provinces and "Hakkaland"

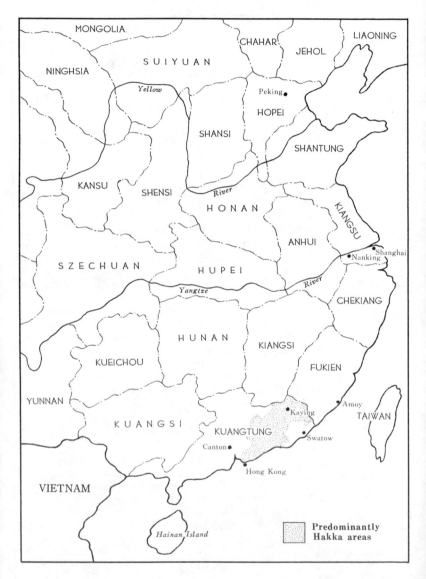

MONGOLIA

LIAONING

CHAHAR

JEHOL

NINGHSIA

SUIYUAN

Yellow

Peking

HOPEI

SHANSI

SHANTUNG

KANSU

SHENSI

River

HONAN

KIANGSU

ANHUI

Shanghai

Nanking

SZECHUAN

HUPEI

River

Yangtze

CHEKIANG

HUNAN

KIANGSI

KUEICHOU

FUKIEN

YUNNAN

Amoy

Kaying

TAIWAN

KUANGSI

KUANGTUNG

Swatow

Canton

Hong Kong

VIETNAM

Hainan Island

Predominantly
Hakka areas

ABOUT THE AUTHOR

David Chia-En Liao, born in 1925 in the southeastern coastal province of Fukien, China, is a grandson of a Congregational pastor. After receiving his Bachelor of Science degree from the missionary-operated Fukien Christian University of Foochow, he went to Taiwan to pursue his career. Through earnest intercession of his devout mother, he experienced a miraculous renewal of faith, and in 1955, answered a definite call to leave his secular occupation to join Overseas Crusades, an American faith mission with headquarters at Santa Clara, California, as a fulltime worker in Taiwan. Among his various responsibilities were teaching discipleship training classes, supervising the Bible Correspondence School, and coordinating citywide crusades and pastors conferences. From 1969 to 1973, he was the director of the Taiwan Field.

Experiences in interdenominational evangelistic work convinced him of the importance of church growth studies. He came to the School of World Mission at Fuller in 1966, but had to interrupt the study to return to his duties in Taiwan. In 1969, when he received the Master of Arts degree in Missions from Fuller, he was also ordained to the ministry of the Gospel. His thesis, dealing with the allegedly resistant Hakka people in Taiwan, was later published by Moody Press and reprinted by the William Carey Library.

In 1955, the same year he began fulltime work with Overseas Crusades, he married Margaret Cheng-Cheng Loh, a coworker in the mission. They now have three teenage children: Peggy, Fred, and Ted.

Books by the
William Carey Library

GENERAL

American Missions in Bicentennial Perspective edited by R. Pierce
    Beaver, $8.95 paper, 448 pp.

The Birth of Missions in America by Charles L. Chaney, $7.95
    paper, 352 pp.

Defeat of the Bird God by C. Peter Wagner, $4.95 paper, 256 pp.

*Education of Missionaries' Children: The Neglected Dimension of
    World Mission* by D. Bruce Lockerbie, $1.95 paper, 76 pp.

Evangelicals Face the Future edited by Donald E. Hoke, $6.95
    paper, 184 pp.

The Holdeman People: The Church in Christ, Mennonite, 1859-1969
    by Clarence Hiebert, $17.95 cloth, 688 pp.

Manual for Accepted Missionary Candidates by Marjorie A. Collins,
    $4.45 paper, 144 pp.

Manual for Missionaries on Furlough by Marjorie A. Collins, $4.45
    paper, 160 pp.

The Ministry of Development in Evangelical Perspective edited by
    Robert L. Hancock, $4.95 paper, 128 pp.

The Night Cometh: Two Wealthy Evangelicals Face the Nation by
    Rebecca J. Winter, $2.95 paper, 96 pp.

*On the Move with the Master: A Daily Devotional Guide on World
    Mission* by Duain W. Vierow, $4.95 paper, 176 pp.

*The Radical Nature of Christianity: Church Growth Eyes Look at
    the Supernatural Mission of the Christian and the Church* by
    Waldo J. Werning (Mandate Press), $5.85 paper, 224 pp.

Social Action Vs. Evangelism: An Essay on the Contemporary Crisis
    by William J. Richardson, $1.95x paper, 64 pp.

The 25 Unbelievable Years: 1945-1969 by Ralph D. Winter, $2.95
    paper, 128 pp.

*The Word-Carrying Giant: The Growth of the American Bible
    Society* by Creighton Lacy, $5.95 paper, 320 pp.

STRATEGY OF MISSION

Church Growth and Christian Mission edited by Donald McGavran,
    $4.95x paper, 256 pp.

Church Growth and Group Conversion by Donald McGavran et al.,
    $2.45 paper, 128 pp.

Committed Communities: Fresh Streams for World Missions by
    Charles J. Mellis, $3.95 paper, 160 pp.

*The Conciliar-Evangelical Debate: The Crucial Documents, 1964-
    1976* edited by Donald McGavran, $8.95 paper, 400 pp.

Crucial Dimensions in World Evangelization edited by Arthur F.
    Glasser et al., $7.95x paper, 512 pp.

Evangelical Missions Tomorrow edited by Wade T. Coggins and
    Edwin L. Frizen, Jr., $5.95 paper, 208 pp.

Everything You Need to Know to Grow a Messianic Synagogue by
    Phillip E. Goble, $2.45 paper, 176 pp.

The Extension Movement in Theological Education: A Call to the Renewal of the Ministry by F. Ross Kinsler, $6.95 paper, 304 pp.

Here's How: Health Education by Extension by Ronald and Edith Seaton, $3.45 paper, 144 pp.

The Indigenous Church and the Missionary by Melvin L. Hodges, $2.95 paper, 108 pp.

Literacy, Bible Reading, and Church Growth Through the Ages by Morris G. Watkins, $4.95 paper, 240 pp.

A Manual for Church Growth Surveys by Ebbie C. Smith, $3.95 paper, 144 pp.

Mission: A Practical Approach to Church-Sponsored Mission Work by Daniel C. Hardin, $4.95x paper, 264 pp.

Readings in Third World Missions edited by Marlin L. Nelson, $6.95x paper, 304 pp.

AREA AND CASE STUDIES

Aspects of Pacific Ethnohistory by Alan R. Tippett, $3.95 paper, 216 pp.

A Century of Growth: The Kachin Baptist Church of Burma by Herman Tegenfeldt, $9.95 cloth, 540 pp.

Christian Mission to Muslims - The Record: Anglican and Reformed Approaches in India and the Near East, 1800-1938 by Lyle L. Vander Werff, $8.95 paper, 384 pp.

The Church in Africa, 1977 edited by Charles R. Taber, $6.95 paper, 224 pp.

Church Growth in Burundi by Donald Hohensee, $4.95 paper, 160 pp.

Church Growth in Japan by Tetsunao Yamamori, $4.95 paper, 184 pp.

The Church in Africa, 1977 edited by Charles R. Taber, $6.95 paper, 224 pp.

Church Planting in Uganda: A Comparative Study by Gailyn Van Rheenen, $4.95 paper, 192 pp.

Circle of Harmony: A Case Study in Popular Japanese Buddhism by Kenneth J. Dale, $4.95 paper, 238 pp.

The Deep-Sea Canoe: The Story of Third World Missionaries in the South Pacific by Alan R. Tippett, $3.45x paper, 144 pp.

Ethnic Realities and the Church: Lessons from India by Donald A. McGavran, $8.95 paper, 272 pp.

The Growth Crisis in the American Church: A Presbyterian Case Study by Foster H. Shannon, $4.95 paper, 176 pp.

The Growth of Japanese Churches in Brazil by John Mizuki, $8.95 paper, 240 pp.

The How and Why of Third World Missions: An Asian Case Study by Marlin L. Nelson, $6.95 paper, 256 pp.

I Will Build My Church: Ten Case Studies of Church Growth in Taiwan edited by Allen J. Swanson, $4.95 paper, 177 pp.

Indonesian Revival: Why Two Million Came to Christ by Avery T. Willis, Jr., $5.95 paper, 288 pp.

Industrialization: Brazil's Catalyst for Church Growth by C.W. Gates, $1.95 paper, 96 pp.

The Navajos are Coming to Jesus by Thomas Dolaghan and David Scates, $4.95 paper, 192 pp.

New Move Forward in Europe: Growth Patterns of German-Speaking Baptists by William L. Wagner, $8.95 paper, 368 pp.

People Movements in the Punjab by Frederick and Margaret Stock,
    $8.95 paper, 388 pp.
Profile for Victory: New Proposals for Missions in Zambia by Max
    Ward Randall, $3.95 cloth, 224 pp.
The Religious Dimension in Hispanic Los Angeles by Clifton L.
    Holland, $9.95 paper, 550 pp.
Solomon Islands Christianity: A Study in Growth and Obstruction
    by Alan R. Tippett, $5.95x paper, 432 pp.
Taiwan: Mainline Vs. Independent Church Growth by Allen J.
    Swanson, $3.95 paper, 300 pp.
Tonga Christianity by Stanford Shewmaker, $3.45 paper, 164 pp.
*Toward Continuous Mission: Strategizing for the Evangelization
    of Bolivia* by W. Douglas Smith, Jr., $4.95 paper, 208 pp.
*Treasure Island: Church Growth Among Taiwan's Urban Minnan
    Chinese* by Robert J. Bolton, $6.95 paper, 416 pp.
Understanding Latin Americans by Eugene Nida, $3.94 paper,
    176 pp.
An Urban Strategy for Africa by Timothy Monsma, $6.95 paper,
    192 pp.
*Worldview and the Communication of the Gospel: A Nigerian Case
    Study* by Marguerite G. Kraft, $7.95 paper, 240 pp.
*A Yankee Reformer in Chile: The Life and Works of David Trum-
    bull* by Irven Paul, $3.95 paper, 172 pp.

APPLIED ANTHROPOLOGY

Becoming Bilingual: A Guide to Language Learning by Donald
    Larson and William Smalley, $5.95x paper, 426 pp.
Christopaganism or Indigenous Christianity? edited by Tetsunao
    Yamamori and Charles R. Taber, $5.95 paper, 242 pp.
*The Church and Cultures: Applied Anthropology for the Religious
    Worker* by Louis J. Luzbetak, $5.95x paper, 448 pp.
*Culture and Human Values: Christian Intervention in Anthropo-
    logical Perspective* (writings of Jacob Loewen) edited by
    William A. Smalley, $5.95x paper, 466 pp.
Customs and Cultures: Anthropology for Christian Missions by
    Eugene A. Nida, $3.95 paper, 322 pp.
Manual of Articulatory Phonetics by William A. Smalley, $5.95x
    paper, 522 pp.
Message and Mission: The Communication of the Christian Faith
    by Eugene A. Nida, $3.95x paper, 254 pp.
Readings in Missionary Anthropology II edited by William A. Smal-
    ley, $9.95x paper, 912 pp.
Religion Across Cultures by Eugene A. Nida, $3.95x paper, 128 pp.
Tips on Taping: Language Recording in the Social Sciences by
    Wayne and Lonna Dickerson, $4.95x paper, 208 pp.

REFERENCE

*Church Growth Bulletin, Second Consolidated Volume (Sept. 1969-
    July 1975)* edited by Donald McGavran, $7.95x paper, 512 pp.
Evangelical Missions Quarterly, Vols. 7-9, $8.95x cloth, 830 pp.
Evangelical Missions Quarterly, Vols. 10-12, $15.95 cloth, 960 pp.
Protestantism in Latin America: A Bibliographical Guide edited by
    John H. Sinclair, $8.95x paper, 448 pp.
Word Study Concordance and New Testament edited by Ralph and
    Roberta Winter, $29.95 cloth, 2-volume set.